ABOUT THE AUTHOR

SJ Murray is an EMMY®-nominated and award-winning writer and producer. Born in Ireland, she works and lives in the US, and is passionate about the roles stories play in shaping culture. A graduate of Auburn, she earned her PhD from Princeton, where she was awarded the Porter Ogden Jacobus Prize as outstanding student of the graduate school, and studied screenwriting at UCLA. As an award-winning tenured professor at Baylor University, SJ is deeply committed to empowering others to become thoughtful writers, grounded in conversations with other writers throughout time. She teaches regularly on story design (a field in which she is recognized as an international pioneer), great texts, leadership & creativity, and screenwriting. Her research has been recognized with fellowships and awards from the American Philosophical Society and National Endowment of the Humanities and has led to widely popular TEDx talks. She has been involved as a speaker, curator, and expert contributor at think tanks and events held at the White House, United Nations, Harvard, the Sorbonne Nouvelle (Paris III), Sundance, and beyond. In addition to films and books, SJ writes short narrative fiction. She lives in Austin, TX with her feisty wheaton-poo, Coco.

BASICS OF
STORY DESIGN

BASICS OF STORY DESIGN

20 STEPS TO AN INSANELY GREAT SCREENPLAY

SJ Murray, PhD

AnderEd
New York

Copyright ©2017 S.J.Murray

All rights reserved. No part of this book may be reproduced or transmitted in any form or by any means, electronic or mechanical, including photocopying, recording, or by any information and storage retrieval system, without expressed written permission from the publisher.

Published in the United States by AnderEd, LLC.

Basicsofstorydesign.com

ISBN: 978-0-692-82330-9

10 9 8 7 6 5 4 3 2 1

First Edition

Preface	1
Getting Started	5
Step 1: Read a Great Script	9
Step 2: Beginnings	11
Step 3: World Building	17
Step 4: Everything Changes	21
Step 5: The Dilemma	27
Step 6: Crossing the Threshold	31
Step 7: A New Friend	35
Step 8: The Midpoint	41
Step 9: All Downhill	45
Step 10: The Grand Finale	53
Step 11: Building Blocks	59
Step 12: Back to Basics	69
Step 13: More Character Basics	77
Step 14: Making a Splash	85
Step 15: Compare and Contrast	89
Step 16: To Outline!	93
Step 17: Please Mind the Gap	99
Step 18: Storytelling Ethics	105
Step 19: To Draft!	113
Step 20: The Rewrite	117
Appendix: Documentary Film	125
Works Cited	137

PREFACE

What is story design? Simply put, it's a term I use to refer to the design process that underlies the crafting of insanely great stories. Although this book is specifically aimed at the story design process for screenwriters, the principles explored here will also be of use to novelists, game designers, and other creative writers seeking to master and implement three-act structure. By popular demand, I've also included an appendix with specific guidelines for documentary filmmakers.

More than a simple outline, story design takes into consideration modern developments in neuroscience research, as well as tried and true methodology for crafting a great story. In this book, I draw from two decades of research into storytelling from the ancient world to modern times, and my own training as a screenwriter and producer of documentary and narrative feature films.

Why another book on screenwriting? There are several good ones. I especially like Richard Walter's *Essentials of Screenwriting*, and had the good fortune of taking several classes in-person from Richard at UCLA. I also draw on principles I learned from Hal Ackerman, and that he shares in *Write Screenplays that Sell.* Joseph Campbell's *Hero with a Thousand Faces*, as well as Christopher Vogler's screenwriting-specific recap in *The Writer's Journey,* are classics, as is Robert McKee's *Story*. Blake Snyder's *Save the Cat!* was the first book on screenwriting that I picked up years ago—and Blake prompted me to deep-dive into the building blocks, or "beats," that make stories work. I've been on that journey ever since and his work served as a springboard for my own pedagogy and writing practices. Blake covers many topics in his book upon which I do not touch. For that reason, I also recommend that you read it. Meanwhile, I've sought to go deeper into the fabric, or DNA, of stories, and to understand *why* certain beats work—and *how*, as opposed to *what* specific elements writers need to execute. My hope is that this book complements other explorations into what it takes to make a good story, by helping writers understand the principles at work beneath the surface of storytelling, so that they can conquer the blank page and do justice to whatever inspired them to write in the first place.

I wrote this book in response to requests from students in my university courses and workshops held from Los Angeles to Paris. They all wanted a portable, simple entry-point into my teachings on story. My goal is to provide a manageable and empowering twenty-step approach to writing an emotionally impactful and marketable dramatic narrative. Day by day, I'll introduce you to basic principles of story design—the very principles I use in my own writing—and guide you through exercises, outlining and drafting until you have a complete draft of your first project. Looking for an accountability partner or for further inspiration? Hop on over to join our writers' community on Facebook in the "Story Design Master Community." You'll find more information and a link at basicsofstorydesign.com, as well as additional worksheets and visual tools.

A word of warning is in order. If you're looking for a magic formula for success, you won't find it here. Designing a great story takes commitment. The crafting of great stories defies convention, and insanely great stories require brute force and countless hours of tedious, invisible work. The best writers outline, draft, write, and rewrite until their labor bears fruit. Master the design process—put in the work it takes to fall nothing short of excellence—and you'll distinguish yourself from the countless aspiring screenwriters and novelists shopping scripts or manuscripts.

Stories have been a huge part of my life for as long as I can remember. I spent my early childhood in the company of Bilbo, Gandalf, Strider, Frodo, and other inspiring characters, who came to life in nightly readings by my father. Between that and visiting ancient castles scattered across Europe, it's no surprise I specialized in medieval literature for my Ph.D. at Princeton University. What later drove me, I think, towards creative writing and filmmaking was not some distaste for the stories of old. On the contrary, they fascinated me and still do. Rather, it was the desire to contribute narratives for our time, and pass on stories to future generations of readers and viewers. As someone once asked me: "If you have the chance to create something of beauty and to send it out into the world to help inform and shape culture, why wouldn't you?"

Before you begin working your way through this book, pause and think about that question. I challenge you to embark upon your quest not in search of fame or fortune, but in the search of something beautiful and crafted with excellence. Stories have the power to change the world. Research has shown that we remember them twenty-two times more than facts. And at their best, stories spark the imagination to transcend time and place, defying the limits of our mortality. They deserve our respect. Medieval writers saw it as a solemn mandate to weave a tapestry of traditions and culture to pass on to future generations. Without our stories, you see, we don't really know who we are. *A civilization that forgets how to tell its story crumbles and dies.*

Deep down inside, I believe we all sense the power of story. From the tales we heard as children, to the narratives constructed by brands and the media today, or the anticipation many of us feel at the release of the next blockbuster movie, we can't help but be impacted by stories. As the research of Paul Zak, Uri Hasson and others has shown, stories impact our brain activity and can even change the chemical balance in our bodies. We are, quite literally, "hardwired for story."

Over the years, meetings with Paul Muldoon and Robert Fagles, begun at Princeton, encouraged me to embrace my creative side and let it soar. Richard Walter and Brian Price significantly enriched the time I spent studying at UCLA and left me with questions I ponder still. I'm grateful to my peers in the NEXUS community, for encouraging me to explore the social impact of film over the past few years and lead conversations from the White House to the United Nations; to the TEDx community for providing me with avenues to talk about such matters publicly; to friends from Summit Series, who taught me not to put off until tomorrow what I can accomplish today; and of course to my colleagues and students at Baylor. Other mentors, friends and family have guided me and I owe to all of them a world of thanks. You know who you are.

This book is for Ronan, my little hero and fighter, capable of surmounting the greatest of odds, and for Declan, the greatest Jedi-in-training the world may ever know.

GETTING STARTED

"I have this idea. It would make a great movie."

Stop right there. Ideas are a dime a dozen. Insanely great ideas? Those take a little more talent and know-how. Having an idea and sitting down in front of your keyboard to birth it on paper couldn't be further removed from what it takes to write even the most basic first draft of a screenplay, although that's a common misconception.

If you've heard me speak, you know that I believe in the power of insanely great stories. Stories are one of the ways we, as human beings, understand who we are and make sense of our place in the world. Stories are at the very core of what it means to be human. As I explained in my 2014 TEDx talk ("Hardwired for Story"), our brains on story behave differently than when they are receiving any other kind of information. That's why story is such a powerful medium.

And yet, not everyone has what it takes to be a great storyteller. Great stories demand hard work and training. That's why so many writers quit before they finish a first draft. Staring at the blank page is so overwhelming and daunting that enthusiasm dwindles and passion fades. They might not even make it beyond page ten. They experience, as Seth Godin puts it, "the dip"—and end the journey.

Writers who abandon their dreams are in part victims of our culture of immediacy, and of the lies we propagate about genius and inspiration. For the record, I've never met a great writer who didn't hit a dip from time to time. Moreover, I've never met a great writer who didn't have to work hard for every word, writing and revising, rethinking and tearing their work to shreds, only to start again at the beginning. Too many first-time writers think storytelling is about getting word-count down on paper, rather than viewing the design of their story as a fundamental and time-consuming process. I'm telling you the truth up front because I don't want you to lose hope, deceived by the illusion that writing is easy. The truth is, it won't be easy. However, it will be worthwhile.

A civilization that forgets how to tell its story crumbles and dies. We *need* great storytellers. We need people willing to put in the time and effort it takes to master the craft. Without the proper tools, those who are eager to embark upon this journey risk getting lost along the way. Still others are committed to the process but don't know where to start. That's why I've written this book.

By learning the basic principles of what I call story design, we're going to empower you to take your project from "Fade In" to "Fade Out." Think of story design and the outlining process as that of constructing a blueprint for your screenplay, similar to the blueprint an architect would prepare for a house. Throughout the process, you'll be able to test, or sound, your blueprint. Missing a load-bearing (story) wall in one spot? We'll catch that before you spend time and resources executing a flawed plan—rather than having to rip that wall down and start over. (Or worse, finding out later that your house is going to fall down.) Far from restricting your creativity, my goal is for you to unleash your creative powers and maximize the time you invest in the writing process.

By going through the process outlined in this book, you should accomplish a pretty decent first draft. It won't be perfect, and like all projects, you'll want to put it through a few more revisions. However, I'm confident when I say that you'll have every opportunity to reach the finish line.

Remember, you'll get out of this 20-step program what you put into it. I'm not only going to guide you through the process of writing your screenplay draft, I'm also going to teach you how to pick up new habits that will empower you to become a better writer. You don't have to complete the challenge in twenty consecutive days. You

Basics of Story Design

can take a break or even just focus on your project a few days a week. You just have to stick with it. It's like going to the gym. You won't see results unless you make the commitment to keep going.

Ready to begin?

- Exercise 1. *Why are you undertaking this 20-step challenge? Take some time to think about it, but don't go any further until you complete this exercise. Self-reflection and motivation are key to follow-through. If you like, you can even copy your reason down on an index card. Pin it above your desk or attach it to your bathroom mirror to remind yourself every day why you're writing in the first place.*

- Exercise 2. *Set aside twenty days in your calendar for learning each of the steps outlined in the following chapters. Be realistic! It's far more motivating and effective to set goals you actually can reach. Stretch yourself a little, but not too much, and keep in mind you don't have to complete each step on consecutive days—you can take some time off for invisible work and other life demands.*

STEP 1. READ A GREAT SCRIPT

You'll never write a great script if you don't read great scripts.

Today, I want you to set aside some time to do just that. You're free to choose any script you wish. Most studios make the scripts nominated for an Academy Award available online for free each year. Choose any script you'd like. Just make sure you're reading the actual script (typically presented as a PDF) and not a transcript.

Here are some options I recommend and that you should be able to find online through a simple search:

- FROZEN (2013)
- CASABLANCA (1942)
- THE MATRIX (1999)
- THE SHAWSHANK REDEMPTION (1994)
- TOY STORY 3 (2010)
- AS GOOD AS IT GETS (1997)
- THE KING'S SPEECH (2010)

In today's exercise, you're going to familiarize yourself with what a great script looks like. You'll also uncover some of the essential elements of insanely great storytelling. Don't fret if you're not sure how to answer the questions. The important thing is that you engage with the script. Before you know it, you'll be reading and analyzing scripts like a pro. Remember, when it comes down to it, you're not going to write a great script if you don't read great scripts.

◆ Exercise 3. *Your reading assignment for today is the first ten pages of the script you selected. You can take notes as you go, but don't answer any of the following questions until you've read the entirety of the first ten pages.*

1. What information do you learn about the setting by the end of page one?
2. What main character is introduced? How? Pay special attention to what this character does when he or she first appears.
3. What is the first event to take place in the movie? What does that event reveal to us about the world of the story?

* From time to time, we'll add script break downs to the Basics of Story Design online community, and host in-person live story design reviews and webinars.

STEP 2. BEGINNINGS

"You either have to write or you shouldn't be writing. That's all."

I couldn't agree more with Joss Whedon. You're probably sitting down to write because of your taste. Stories excite you and stretch your imagination. Perhaps they offer a much-needed escape from reality. It's your taste for, and love of, good stories that's getting you into this game—and if it's not, you might want to reconsider.

Writing isn't about achieving fame or fortune. It's not about calling attention to yourself. Come to think of it, can you recall seeing many writers interviewed by the paparazzi outside awards shows lately?

Chances are, you'll become discouraged somewhere along your journey. It's inevitable. As Ira Glass reminds us, "Your taste is what disappoints you." Sooner or later, you're going to realize that your earliest writings don't measure up to your taste. That can be a brutal and disappointing realization. You may succumb to self-doubt. Many of you will even consider quitting and wonder what made you think you could succeed in the first place. (Your protagonist will go through a similar process until he or she pushes through the Brick Wall, as we'll see later in this book.) When that time comes, you must push through. Over time and with practice, you're going to close the gap between taste and ability. It's going to be hard work and take a lot of sustained effort. But if you stick with it, you'll get there.

Today we're going to talk about beginnings. Beginnings are

important for many reasons. The opening of your movie will win over or lose the audience, just like that. When it comes to writing a spec script—that is, a script you intend to pitch to a producer or studio—beginnings are also crucial for winning over your reader. Readers have so many scripts assigned to them every week that they won't read beyond the first page if you don't grab their interest right away. No lie. If you can convince them to turn to page two, they'll probably stick with the script until page five. If they make it to page five, they're likely read on to page ten. And so on.

When it comes to structuring your story, the beginning is important because it's the foundation upon which the whole of the adventure rests. Develop a flimsy foundation and the whole story falls down. With this in mind, let's take a closer look at how to craft a great *point of attack* or *opening image*.

Every story begins somewhere. Get in too early and the audience gets lost in the mundane details of the character and becomes frustrated when they have no idea where your story is going. Get in too late, and they can't grasp how much the life of your character is turned upside down when the *inciting incident* or *catalyst* occurs (see Chapter 4). For all of these reasons, it's absolutely crucial to pick the right place to begin.

Every writer will develop his or her techniques in deciding what the opening image should be. Most brainstorm several possibilities and settle on the one that sets the story up best. Sometimes, you may have a clear vision from the very start of a project. Other times, as your story grows and takes on a life of its own, it cries out for an entirely different beginning. The key, as a writer, is to be flexible as the story comes into focus. When brainstorming a new story, I always think about where I want to leave the viewer at the end. That helps me sort out the significant themes driving the conflict and what values are at stake. I may not know exactly how I'll get to that ending or precisely what the climax looks like, but I do have some sense of how the tensions at work in my story resolve themselves.

Michael Arndt—writer of LITTLE MISS SUNSHINE (2006), TOY STORY 3 (2010) and STAR WARS VII: THE FORCE AWAKENS (2015)—once told me that writing a script is a lot like playing golf. If you can't see the green or the flag in the hole, you don't know how to aim your shot. In this sense screenwriting is very different from, say, writing a poem. Begin with the end in mind and you'll successfully create your most important tent-pole moment.

You don't have to know all the details surrounding how the climax plays out. It's enough to know it involves a showdown between the antagonist and protagonist, or that the protagonist will make the ultimate sacrifice for the greater good. At this stage of the process, you don't have to know exactly how it happens or how you get there —just that it *will* happen.

When you begin with the end in mind, something magical happens. The conflicting values of the story world come into focus. Ultimately, these values may also change. As ideas play out and characters evolve, you might end up taking the story in an entirely different direction. That's the point of a first draft—to find out where you're going. In the rewrites, you can hone and fine-tune the story.

The tension between underdog and dominant values fuels the central conflict of great stories. In his *Art of Dramatic Writing*, Lajos Egri calls this principle the dramatic premise. There's a lot of confusion around this term and on numerous occasions, I've encountered writers who adopt the term "premise" to refer to a brief summary of the plot, synonymous with a *logline*. Over the course of this book, I want you to learn to think of the premise of your story in terms of the values at stake, the way Egri defines it. It's that tension that empowers you to design an insanely great story and build suspense over the three-act structure.

Underdog values are those at risk in the world when we enter into it. They are jeopardized by the dominant values of society, often embodied by the antagonist: "Great love transcends death." "Hope succumbs to pride." "Freedom triumphs over tyranny." There are as many premises as there are great stories to be told. Let's take a closer look at a few examples.

In the climax of the original STAR WARS IV: A NEW HOPE (1977), Luke gives in to his belief in the mysterious Force. Against all odds, he destroys the Death Star despite the technological superiority of the evil Empire. Good, and everything the rebellion represents (freedom, justice and courage...), triumphs over evil, oppression, and servitude.

Randall Wallace ends BRAVEHEART (1995) on the death of William Wallace. Wallace stands firm for freedom and self-sacrifice in the face of great adversity. He understands that revenge was never enough. His commitment to a higher calling in the storybook world inspires future generations of Scotsmen, and solidifies a vision for sacrificial leadership.

The first scene of THE PATRIOT (2000) reveals a tomahawk locked away in a chest. The voice of Benjamin Martin hints that the past, and everything the weapon represents, are coming back to haunt him. That particular image stays with us throughout the first act. It causes us to wonder, along with Martin's sons, what happened in the Wilderness. The tomahawk signals that THE PATRIOT is a movie about war. It also creates a dramatic tension with what we uncover on-screen about Martin turned gentleman farmer, striving to make the perfect rocking chair in his plantation barn, far away from the brewing conflict.

Finally, another example to which I often return to identify the qualities of a great opening scene is KRAMER VS. KRAMER (1979). The story centers on workaholic Ted Kramer, who struggles to become a good father when his wife, Joanna, leaves him. Joanna comes back for their child and Ted must fight for custody. The opening is chilling. We meet a jubilant Ted on his way home after being given a promotion. Meanwhile, Joanna waits alone, chain-smoking in their apartment living room. We know this because the ashtray beside her is full of cigarettes. Ted enters and goes straight to the phone to make a business call. While he's on the phone, Joanna announces she's leaving him.

We barely see Joanna pack her suitcase. When Ted arrives, it stands ready at the door. The audience enters the narrative at a critical moment: Joanna walks out, leaving her son behind. In the span of three minutes, the audience grasps everything there is to know about Ted and Joanna's failed marriage. We infer the years of fighting and hurt. Please remember this capital rule of great storytelling, and great story rhetoric: *Show, don't tell.*

Creating a multi-dimensional opening scene takes a lot of brainstorming, writing, and rewriting. We'll learn more about crafting great scenes later in the series. For now, focus on what's at stake when we meet your protagonist. What does she want? What does she need? How is she blind to that need and how does her blindness affect others? Above all, avoid the temptation to pack the suitcase.

Got that? Don't forget to read back over your notes from today before going to bed. Research shows that if you do, you'll retain around 70% more of the information you've learned.

- Exercise 4. *Let's recap and think about how to apply everything you've learned today to the story you want to write.*

    1. What effect must the opening image of a movie achieve? Why? Provide specific examples.
    2. Explain what sets of values are at stake in the premise of a story.
    3. In the story you're about to tell, what would the values and the premise be?

- Exercise 5. *Now is a good time to revisit the script you're reading.*

    1. Read back through the opening ten pages or so and think about how the opening image sets the stage for the entire story. What are some of the techniques adopted by the writer?
    2. Why do you think those techniques are successful?

STEP 3. WORLD BUILDING

Soon, very soon, something is going to happen.

The protagonist just doesn't know it yet. The opening scene carries us through the first three minutes of the movie—that's three pages in typical script format. Sometimes it's shorter, sometimes it's longer, but the job of the opening scene is to ensure the audience has a sense of what the movie's going to be about, and what's at stake. In the pages and scenes that follow, the writer must introduce the protagonist and the ordinary world to set the stage for the story.

- In STAR WARS IV: A NEW HOPE, Darth Vader's invasion of the rebel starship and the capture of Princess Leia show us immediately that we're in space, and at war. We grasp that the rebels are fighting against a tyrannical Empire. Turn off the volume, and we still understand what's at stake. The struggle between makeshift rebellion and all-powerful Empire is expressed right down to the design of the beat-up rebel spaceship and the massive, technologically advanced Imperial starship.

- By the end of the first scene of FINDING NEMO (2003), Marlin loses his wife and 399 children. He cups the sole remaining egg in his fin and promises always to take care of... Nemo. That, of course, is what the whole movie is about. When Nemo is abducted, Marlin does whatever it takes to find him. We also understand—because we understand

Marlin's past—just how great a loss he feels. Losing Nemo is Marlin's worst nightmare. He relives the most traumatic loss he ever experienced. Nemo is all Marlin has left. (Pause here to shed a tear. This story gets our emotions going!)

The important thing to remember about the ordinary world or "world as we know it" is that we are encountering the protagonist as he or she goes about business as usual. Very soon something is going to happen—but the protagonist doesn't know it yet. Even when a character bends the rule and anticipates change, like Tony in WEST SIDE STORY (1961), he only has a vague sense, or perhaps a premonition, that something unusual is coming.

At the beginning of Act One, we meet the protagonist's friends, find out what defines ordinary life for the character and discover rivalries or other sources of conflict. Little by little, the protagonist's character is revealed by the decisions she makes and the ways she interacts with others—but not because a character verbalizes what the well-intentioned novice thinks the audience should know at the beginning of the story (the no-no known as "exposition"). We discover the protagonist's nature by watching her live her life.

Let's talk some more about exposition. In a memorable scene near the beginning of PULP FICTION (1994), we meet the two hit men played by Samuel L. Jackson and John Travolta. They are nonchalantly driving along, chatting aimlessly. Screenwriting expert Richard Walter will tell you that you should avoid car scenes as much as restaurants. He's right, because these kinds of scenarios breed exposition. Tarantino, however, is a master craftsman. Watch, and admire.

In PULP FICTION, the characters philosophize about seemingly trite topics: whether it's okay or not to give the boss's wife a foot rub, what a quarter pounder with cheese is called in France. They park the car, grab guns from the trunk, and execute the soulless massacre of drug dealers who have been encroaching on their boss's territory. Whoa.

The novice writer might have weighed down the story with useless and meaningless expository dialogue. "Hey, man, can you believe this is our fiftieth hit together?" "How long have we been doing this, anyhow?" "Remember that one time...at band camp?" (Just kidding.) Instead, what Tarantino achieves is masterful. When the hit men chat about all kinds of things irrelevant to the task at hand—food in Paris, giving foot rubs—he reveals to us how cold-blooded they are. *This* is their ordinary world. Parking a car, pulling out guns and mowing down some amateurs who have overstepped their boundaries is as second nature to these guys as taking my dog for a walk is to me. It's jarring. Without telling us a single thing about the moral worldview of the characters, Tarantino shows us everything we need to know. That's filmmaking at its best.

Here's another example of how a story can set up the ordinary world and reveal character through action. In THE PROPOSAL (2009), Margaret Tate is a go-getter career girl and workaholic. We know this because when the movie begins, she is up before dawn in her fancy Manhattan apartment, cycling on her stationary bike, reading a manuscript, half-heartedly watching an intense woodsy simulator on her TV. Margaret's job is her world. We wonder if she has ever bothered to notice the breathtaking—real—view of Central Park we see right outside her window.

That is how a great set up sequence—the ordinary world—functions. By experiencing a tiny slice of Margaret's life, we surmise all kinds of things about her. Within minutes, we feel like we know Margaret, even though she hasn't said a word.

Andrew Paxton, meanwhile, is quite the opposite—or is he? Andrew lives in a small, simple apartment. He oversleeps and doesn't have time to date. (According to an earlier version of the script, he doesn't even have time to remember the name of the girl beside him when he wakes up.) He, too, is enslaved by his job, driven to succeed at all cost. Andrew knows that in order to succeed, he must please his boss, Margaret, even though he loathes her. No one likes Margaret. We know this because as she approaches the office, Andrew fires off a warning email to everyone on staff: "The wicked witch is on the broom."

As the scene unfolds, we learn that Andrew will do anything for a promotion. Margaret will do anything to keep her job. When disaster strikes, it's hardly surprising that the reckless determination inherent to both of these characters is completely believable, since the audience feels like they already know and fully understand their laser-focused, workaholic existences. We know what drives them: success at any cost.

Of course, Andrew fails to realize that part of him is just like Margaret. Each views the other only as a means to an end...but you'll have to watch the movie to find out what happens. (If you want to get the most out of this experience, make the time to watch the movies discussed in each step.)

♦ Exercise 6. *Let's recap and brainstorm.*

1. Describe the sequence of scenes that occurs after the opening image in your chosen script. What's the purpose of this sequence?
2. Name three key characteristics of the ordinary world of the story you desire to communicate in the opening ten pages of your script.
3. In the script that you're reading, list at least three things you learn about the main character and his or her world during the opening ten pages. How does the writer convey this information?

STEP 4. EVERYTHING CHANGES

The inciting incident becomes a pivotal moment in your character's life.

Today we'll learn about the *inciting incident* (also known as the *catalyst*). This is the moment when the story takes a major turn. An example of an inciting incident is when Peter Parker gets bitten by a spider (**SPIDER-MAN**, 2002). He doesn't know it yet, but the venom is about to give him superpowers.

First, a few comments on the importance of *point of view* (POV). In general, movies that are successful at the box office are driven by the narrative POV of one character. This person is your protagonist. The story revolves around the things that happen to provoke a profound change in the protagonist—even if that change comes through encountering another person. Look, for example, at the character of Antonio Salieri in **AMADEUS** (1984). His life is profoundly impacted by his meeting Mozart. Yet, the movie is very much Salieri's story and told from his POV.

While movies with multiple POVs do exist (they are known as *multiplots*), they tend to be less successful at the box office. That's not because audiences are brainwashed by the Hollywood model, mind you. Nor is it because the average audience member lacks intelligence or taste. Simply put, by immersing the audience in one single POV, they develop an emotional attachment to the story—the audience feels what the character feels.

When the protagonist's POV is clear, we root for or against her. We fear for her safety. We hang on to the hope the world can still be saved. Watch **FINDING NEMO** or **HOW TO TRAIN YOUR DRAGON** 2 (2014) to see what I mean. Both movies draw the audience in so well that we forget we're not watching actual fish or dragons in danger, but a collection of animated pixels. That's because the emotions we feel are real. When the story is well told, the audience becomes a part of it. We don't simply suspend disbelief, we forget about the so-called "real" world and become immersed in the world of the story.

I won't focus in this book on the art of the multiplot. Instead, you'll learn to write a strong, single POV movie. Be thinking over the next day or two about some of the defining traits of your protagonist. We'll return to such considerations a little further down the road.

Back to the inciting incident. This is the first major story beat, or twist, in your plot. We'll illustrate the inciting incident by taking another look at **THE PROPOSAL**.

Margaret is on top of the world, working her dream job and devoting herself entirely to her career. She's so darn busy doing what it takes to succeed at work that she doesn't have time for such paltry things as verifying her visa status. Who cares about those kinds of details?

The day we meet Margaret and Andrew, everything changes—for both of them, since we're in the midst of a romantic comedy (but the story remains primarily hers). Margaret drives the action.

It's important to understand the difference between what the writer knows and what the characters know. As the inciting incident approaches, the writer knows exactly what's coming. Everything is about to change. The audience suspects this too; they've seen plenty of movies. It's paramount, however, that your characters not realize that someone is just about to light a stick of dynamite underneath them.

Keep in mind, as you move forward with your story, that what you want and seek to accomplish as a writer must be kept quite separate from what your characters know and want. Every time your protagonist walks out the door, she must face very real decisions in the most believable way possible, driven by what she is seeking to accomplish. This is what writers call the character's *desire line*.

At the beginning of every scene, ask yourself, "What does my character want? How is this different from what I am seeking to accomplish as a writer?" And then keep those goals separate. Doing so will help you avoid the dreaded coincidence (e.g., your character decides to go somewhere because you, the author, need her to).

So, how does all of this play out in THE PROPOSAL? Margaret goes in to work. We have a good sense by now of how she is as a person and as a boss. In spite of her character flaws, we also get the sense that she's good at her job. It's very much in character, then, that she congratulates herself upon getting the message to come up and speak with her bosses. Margaret has a one-track mind. She has landed a great writer—perhaps one of the greatest coups of her career—and she fully expects to be lavished with praise and kudos for a job well done. Time to pour the champagne, even if it is before lunch. Margaret has positively no idea what's about to happen.

Imagine her surprise when she discovers she's being let go. It seems there's a problem with her U.S. visa. They're sending her back to Canada. But Margaret will not allow it. Note that fighting back is a believable and established trait of her personality, too. Quick to think, she announces her engagement to an equally surprised Andrew. Since the fate of his own publishing career rests in Margaret's hands, Andrew goes along with her lie, if somewhat reluctantly.

There is much to be gleaned about writing from this pivotal moment of THE PROPOSAL. As a writer, you must learn to play with the boundary between what your character knows vs. what the audience knows. As we watch THE PROPOSAL, the audience is well aware that Margaret is making up her engagement to Andrew. Because of this, we experience Andrew's shock, discomfort and strained attempt to play along. We also know that Margaret's bosses are out of the loop. The gap between what we know and what they know creates comic relief. Moreover, it builds suspense. How will Margaret pull off the subterfuge? How will Andrew respond once they're in private? The stick of dynamite is lit and the fuse is burning —but it hasn't exploded yet.

NOTTING HILL (1999) deals with the inciting incident in a

slightly different, although equally endearing, way. The movie opens with the voice of William Thacker, an unsuccessful bookstore owner in the Notting Hill section of London. William introduces us to his neighborhood, the storybook world. He reveals that today is the day everything changes for him. (We presume the narrator must be looking back, recounting the events after the fact.)

William's pronouncement sets the stage for the inciting incident. What's about to happen that will change his life forever? Anna Scott, the most famous movie star in the world, walks into his little shop. Again, the stick of dynamite is lit. Note, however, that William makes no attempt to ask her for her number at this time. That comes a little later when he bumps into her in the street and spills orange juice all over her. The "meet cute" (the moment when the boy meets the girl) in the shop sets everything in motion. In that scene, the seeds of the possible romance are sown.

The principle of not allowing the characters to know what happens next is well implemented here, too. When Anna walks out of the shop, William is sure he'll never see her again. He goes out to get coffee and to unwind—not to look for her. Similarly, in STAR WARS IV: A NEW HOPE, Luke stumbles across his destiny when he is looking for it the least, as he follows his uncle's instructions and prepares to wipe the memories of the two droids they just acquired from the Jawas. Nothing prepares Luke for what he finds: Princess Leia's distress message concealed by R2D2. The message sets in motion Luke's quest. It makes real and palpable a simple farm boy's call to greatness. After seeing Leia's message, Luke cannot shake the possibility the droid might have belonged to someone he knows, old Ben Kenobi. He's driven to investigate this mystery, yet has no idea about the adventure upon which he's about to embark.

In all of these examples, the inciting incident lights the fuse—and it burns until the stick of dynamite explodes. Remember, the inciting incident needn't be the most mind-blowing change in the world (although it could be). Rather, it serves as a catalyst for the journey ahead, setting in motion the irreversible and inevitable process of change.

Basics of Story Design

◆   Exercise 7. *Let's go back to the script you selected to read. Review the initial twenty pages.*
1. Can you spot the inciting incident? Describe in detail how the scene unfolds.
2. Identify one way the writer set up the inciting incident. How does the writer make this scene believable? How does it shake up the ordinary world?
3. How does the protagonist initially react to the inciting incident?

STEP 5. THE DILEMMA

Should I stay or should I go?

That's pretty much how I like to think of the *dilemma* moment. Whatever the inciting incident set in motion, the dilemma brings to the forefront. The dilemma is also known as the seventeen-minute point because in a two-hour movie, the dilemma tends to hurl itself onto the screen at seventeen minutes in. Here, the stick of dynamite explodes and the protagonist faces an unavoidable moment of questioning: to reject, or accept, the invitation to go on the quest.

In STAR WARS IV: A NEW HOPE, the inciting incident, as we have seen, consists of R2D2 revealing part of Leia's message to Luke. However, the stick of dynamite explodes when R2 plays back the whole message for Obi-Wan, revealing the Empire's drive to destroy the rebellion and their only hope. Unless the plans concealed in the R2 unit reach Alderaan and Leia's father discovers some kind of weakness in the Empire's weapon system, the rebellion will be wiped out.

Luke now finds himself in the midst of the conflict. Obi-Wan invites him to travel to Alderaan to deliver the plans. The old Jedi Master goes so far as to explain Luke's father was also a Jedi Knight, who knew the ways of the Force. As proof and a final nudge, Obi-Wan gives Luke his father's old light saber—the weapon of the Jedi. (If you've read Christopher Vogler's *Writer's Journey*, you'll recognize that the light saber is Luke's *talisman*. Meanwhile, Luke's mentor figure, Obi-Wan, plays the role of *threshold guardian*.)

Like all heroes, Luke resists the call. He can't possibly go to

Alderaan. His uncle needs him; the harvest's coming; there's too much work to be done at home. How far we have come from that opening dinner scene when Luke squabbled with his uncle about not being able to go to the academy! Dreaming about being a great fighter pilot and going to the academy is, to be fair, a whole lot simpler than finding oneself smack in the middle of war and in possession of plans the Empire is seeking to retrieve at all cost.

What we witness in this scene is the conflict between Luke's *internal stakes* (Will he become a Jedi Knight? Will he answer that call to greatness?) and the *external stakes*, embodied by the all-powerful Empire, poised to quash the rebels like insects. Luke faces, very literally, a dilemma. What should he do? Should he stay or should he go? At the first opportunity, Luke retreats.

Let's consider another example. In GLADIATOR (2000), the inciting incident is Marcus Aurelius's charge to Maximus: Become the protector of Rome, rule in Commodus's place and give Rome back to the people. Let Rome be restored to her glory and be a Republic once more. Maximus's desire to return home and see his family stands in direct opposition to his call to go to Rome and take a stand for the future of the great city in which he believes. The fuse is lit. Of course, General Maximus refuses the call and the emperor gives him until nightfall to think it over. Oh hesitation, at what cost you come! During those few hours, Commodus learns Maximus is to rule in his place, murders his father and claims the throne.

Maximus's dilemma occurs when the new emperor summons him. Suspense is at an all-time high. Will Maximus pledge allegiance to Commodus? Or will he smell a rat? To make matters worse, Maximus has already made up his mind to serve Marcus Aurelius and go to Rome. (We know this because he tells his slave, Cicero, they may not be able to go home after all.) But it's too late. The disjuncture between what we know, and what the protagonist knows, fuels the suspense. We've seen Commodus kill Marcus Aurelius with our very own eyes. Thus, while Maximus is surprised to find himself face to face with a new emperor, we are not.

The setting opens up an opportunity for the audience to focus, instead, on what is central to the story: Maximus's reaction to the events. Commodus presents his hand and ring, asking for Maximus to declare his allegiance...but the general refuses it and goes to his quarters to arm himself. Although Maximus hesitated when he was presented with the inciting incident, he responds decisively at the so-called seventeen-minute point, or dilemma. But it's too late. The die is cast. That's the stuff of which great tragedies—and great underdog heroes—are made.

Here's another way to think of the dilemma. The inciting incident shakes things up, but like all of us, the protagonist may not respond eagerly to change. Perhaps, even, she just doesn't understand yet the significance of the inciting incident. After all, she's experiencing the events as they unfold. As I've already pointed out, the protagonist has no idea what's coming next. Something may seem different at the inciting incident, but it's only upon looking back that the protagonist would be able to say, "That's where it all started, right there."

The dilemma, on the other hand, makes the events of the inciting incident palpable and unavoidable. There's no denying that everything is changing. Still, the protagonist doesn't make the leap right into the abyss and the unknown. What's different and significant is that she can no longer avoid the changes taking place around her. The *decision*—the commitment to move forward in the story—looms just around the corner. The protagonist must come to terms with the invitation into the adventure of the story world. She may resist at first, but eventually something's going to happen to make that resistance futile. That something creates the dilemma. The protagonist can no longer put off making a decision. She must face the reality that a choice must be made.

As you now understand, the inciting incident and dilemma work together to create tension. Remember, the goal is for tension to increase gradually over the course of the story. That's what we call *rising conflict*. So the call to adventure must be even more pressing at the dilemma than it was during the inciting incident. Keep in mind also that your job is always to show and not tell. Your protagonist cannot tell us how she is feeling or that danger is imminent. Instead, we must see it. This means that the inciting incident and dilemma will most likely be set in motion by external circumstances that affect the protagonist. Your job, as a writer, is to figure out how your protagonist reacts. That's one of the foundational elements of every scene.

At its most basic, a scene consists of a *setup* (i.e., what is going on at the beginning of the scene) followed by an *event* to which the protagonist reacts or refuses to react. (Refusal is an action in and of itself.) Then the other characters in the scene react to the protagonist's reaction. Or vice-versa. We'll have plenty of occasions to dig deeper into the art of crafting scenes. For now, let's round out the day with an exercise.

♦ Exercise 8. *Look over your notes from yesterday. Review the inciting incident in the script you're reading.*

1. Is there a corresponding dilemma? (Don't worry if there isn't one. Some movies don't develop this beat.)
2. How does the pairing of the inciting incident and dilemma reinforce the stakes of the movie and its premise?
3. Get creative! Brainstorm two or three original inciting incident/ dilemma pairings.
4. Continue reading your selected script to page 40. Be sure to take notes and watch out for key moments that contribute to the protagonist's ongoing character development.

STEP 6. CROSSING THE THRESHOLD

There is no turning back.

Sooner or later—and, in the case of a well-crafted blockbuster-style movie, right at the end of Act One (or around twenty-five to twenty-seven pages into the script)—the protagonist must commit whole-heartedly to the adventure. This might be a quest to save the world, a burgeoning romance, or even a dance competition. The goal must be real and it must be tangible. By tangible, I mean that whatever the protagonist is seeking, everyone in the audience should be able to agree about what it looks like for her to accomplish and achieve (or fail to achieve) that goal. Perhaps the missing treasure is returned to the chest, or the national championship is won or, even, the bomb is defused.

What the protagonist is after, in movie lingo, is referred to as the "broomstick," in homage to the great WIZARD OF OZ (1939), or the "MacGuffin," a term popularized by Alfred Hitchcock and possibly inspired by his screenwriter friend Angus MacPhail. Hitchcock explained how this device works in a lecture at Columbia University in 1939: "We have a name in the studio and we call it the MacGuffin. It is the mechanical element that usually crops up in any story. In crook stories it is almost always the necklace, and in spy stories it is most always the papers." So, thinking of what Hitchcock said here, whatever it might be, the MacGuffin is the main driving force of the movie—or at the very least it appears to be by the end of Act One. Deliver the plans to Alderaan; save Elizabeth from pirates; win the cheerleading competition. There are as many possible

MacGuffins as there are stories to tell.

The MacGuffin is equally relevant in stories about inner transformation. That said, an inner transformation is exceedingly hard to depict on screen. It's far simpler for your protagonist to make decisions that are the result of an inner transformation, so as to accomplish (or fail to accomplish) a tangible goal. In striving to accomplish the goal, the obstacles thrown in the protagonist's path, the decisions she must make and the actions she performs on screen, make the inner transformation clear to the audience. Again, we're back to our number one rule: Show, don't tell. Think about SILVER LININGS PLAYBOOK (2012), a story of intense inner conflicts and transformations. The MacGuffin is a dance competition, for which the stakes are raised by the bet.

It's insufficient for your protagonist to claim she has changed; she needs a tangible goal to pursue, and pursuing that very goal makes the character transformation possible. The pursuit pushes and stretches the protagonist to the point that transformation is inevitable.

The first act break occurs when the protagonist makes a commitment to pursue the perceived goal and crosses over from the ordinary world to the extraordinary world. (Christopher Vogler has great thoughts about this transition, which he calls the "threshold," in his *Writer's Journey*.)

Of course, there doesn't necessarily come a point in the narrative that the protagonist achieves the goal. If she does, she'll probably reach it in an unexpected way. Or perhaps she achieves that goal just to find out an even greater one is at stake. In PIRATES OF THE CARIBBEAN: THE CURSE OF THE BLACK PEARL (2003), Will Turner sets out to save Elizabeth and find out the identity of his father. The subsequent quest to return the gold coin to the chest is uncovered while Will is already on his original journey. In other words, Will sets out to accomplish one goal. In the process of pursuing it, he uncovers another overarching goal. In *Writing Screenplays That Sell*, Michael Hauge considers this process of uncovering the true goal to be one of the most important elements in building your story. I think he's right.

One of Michael's favorite examples of this process at work—and one of my faves, too—is SHREK (2001). Shrek's swamp is invaded by fairy creatures and he sets out to visit Lord Farquaad to have them removed. It's in the process of completing this initial quest that Shrek uncovers his true quest: to save the princess (with whom he falls in love) and protect her at all cost from Farquaad, who sent him off to seek her in the first place.

Thus, the protagonist may commit to a goal only to discover later that what she is really after—the MacGuffin or broomstick—is something else altogether.

It's also important to note that, in order to cross over from Act One into Act Two, the protagonist cannot simply be carried along by the unfolding events. Obi-Wan cannot drag Luke to Alderaan. Instead, Luke uncovers the death of his family and makes the decision, alone, to follow Obi-Wan and enter the extraordinary world. In a similar vein, Snow White cannot be swept out of the castle drains and over the ledge in SNOW WHITE AND THE HUNTSMAN (2012). She holds herself on the ledge, hesitates, looks back, and makes the proactive decision to jump. And in THE PATRIOT, Benjamin Martin witnesses the murder of his middle son, who dies in his arms. Reminiscent of William Wallace in BRAVEHEART, Benjamin goes into a calculated frenzy of revenge. He runs upstairs, claims his talisman (the mysterious tomahawk), and sets out to massacre the British to free his eldest son. As in the other examples we have seen, Benjamin responds proactively to the events and circumstances by making a decision to enter the conflict.

In principle, then, crossing over always demands a decisive act of commitment. This holds true even if later on the protagonist is likely to discover that she has committed to something greater than she could possibly have realized at the end of Act One.

- ◆ Exercise 9. *Let's take a little time to review how the writer develops the protagonist in the script you're reading and how the character commits to crossing the threshold into Act Two.*

1. What drives the protagonist?
2. How is this taken away from the protagonist?
3. What is your character's want? How is that want established by the writer using *show, don't tell* ?
4. What is the protagonist's need? Is there something that happened to create that need?
5. Where does the act break (i.e., the transition from Act One into Act Two) occur? Why does the protagonist commit to crossing the threshold?

STEP 7. A NEW FRIEND

Welcome to the extraordinary world.

Once the protagonist crosses over, it's time to discover the extraordinary world. This sets in motion the story movement I like to call the "adventure sequence."

It takes a little time to get acquainted with all the rules and customs of the new world. Just as we discovered the protagonist's everyday world at the beginning of Act One, we now get to discover the extraordinary world, where the bulk of the adventure will unfold. If the story promises to be about pirates, it's time for lots of pirates, ships, and curses to be broken as we sail around the ocean. If it's about space, then we had best commandeer a ship and make the jump into hyperspace, or explore distant solar systems in search of a new planet on which humanity can start over. If it's a romance, then we're into the heart of the quest for love.

Sometimes, "crossing over" takes place after the protagonist plays around with his newfound powers. Take ABOUT TIME (2013), for example. Tim's father, Bill, reveals to him that the men in their family all have the ability to travel within their own timeline. When Tim tries this out, he discovers it's no joke. Tim's initial reaction is that he will use the power to find love. However, as the dilemma sequence shows us, it won't be quite as simple as Tim thinks. The complications of real life are not eradicated by time travel. It's not until Tim crosses over and moves to London to stay with his father's friend that he meets Mary, his future wife, in Act Two. As a result of that encounter, he begins to use his powers purposefully.

It's worth keeping in mind the following principle as you develop the adventure sequence: For a while, there's no reason to raise the stakes. The story and protagonist need time to find their legs in the new world. During the first act, the protagonist confronted a number of key changes. Now it's time to relax and get our bearings. During the adventure sequence, the protagonist is also likely to make good progress towards achieving her goal. We all know that moment, sitting in the movie theatre, when we think to ourselves: "This is too easy... I just know something bad is going to happen." And that's precisely the rhetorical effect of the adventure sequence. By slowing things down and allowing the protagonist to make progress, the writer builds anticipation for the next major twist and turn the protagonist will encounter at the midpoint.

For me, two significant (and closely related) events take place during the adventure sequence, and define it. First, the protagonist meets the supporting character shortly after Act Two begins. If we want to get technical, I think this encounter needs to happen by page 30 or 35 in the script—that's approximately one third of the way through the story. (Sometimes, in love stories, it happens much earlier—around the catalyst point. That doesn't preclude a friend being introduced as a subplot driver in Act Two.) What makes the new character the supporting (or "B") character is this: His primary purpose is to support the protagonist in moving forward through the character arc. If we view the protagonist's character arc over the course of the story much like an old stone vault in a medieval cathedral, then the supporting character is the keystone at the center of the vault. Without it, the arc could not hold itself up. The noticeable differences between supporting character and protagonist allow the latter to understand her own worldview and choices. In some cases, the protagonist emulates the supporting character's worldview or actions. In others, she reacts against them. Of course, all stories can (and often do) have more than one subplot.

For example, in STAR WARS IV: A NEW HOPE, Obi-Wan, Han Solo and Princess Leia all play key roles in fueling Luke's inner journey: Obi-Wan as mentor, Han Solo as his newfound friend and comrade (and rival), and Princess Leia as (initially) the love interest.

At the end of the day, Han is the key supporting character once Luke crosses into Act Two. Han is completely different from Luke. He's a smuggler. Much like Rick in CASABLANCA (1942), Han doesn't stick his neck out for anyone; he's concerned with his own interests. Initially, the external stakes of the story mean little to him. Han's personality also conflicts with Luke's on other levels. On the philosophical level, Han buys into a realistic, self-imposed system of justice. He lives outside the mainstream. Good vs. evil may be idealistic, but for him, the notion doesn't pan out in day-to-day existence. Han clashes with the internal stakes, too. He doesn't believe in the Force and questions Luke's calling. Interestingly, Han's questioning is precisely what Luke needs to break through and embrace the Force himself. By the end of the story, Han also becomes Luke's decisive ally. Han, too, grows from the friendship. He returns to save his friend when Luke needs him the most. In this give-and-take between himself and Han, Luke learns to assert, define, and articulate his own very singular identity. That's what makes Han Solo a great supporting character.

The second defining event I pay attention to in this part of the story occurs before the midpoint, when the protagonist does something she would not have done in Act One. This is oftentimes referred to as the forty-minute point. (Like the seventeen-minute point, it need not occur precisely at forty minutes. However, it should occur after meeting the supporting character and before the midpoint.) The importance of this beat is to show us something has changed. The protagonist no longer finds herself where she was at the end of Act One. Because of this early step towards transformation, she attempts something she never would have done before. Perhaps it's due to the encouragement of the supporting character, or perhaps it's in defiance—in any case, it's a direct result of the events that have taken place so far in the story.

The protagonist may or may not succeed. The point, simply, is that she tries. Something has changed and we get the sense that the adventure has truly begun. (You'll find it useful to include a repeat of this character beat around the 60-minute point as well, or sometime during the second half of Act Two. This time, the protagonist will do something she would never have done during the first half of Act Two.)

By creating a supporting character different in some key way from your protagonist, you'll bring a new dimension of conflict into your story that will help fuel the second act. It also challenges the protagonist to grow through the character arc.

The conflict introduced will not be resolved until later. That's because you must keep building it up in order to maintain the audience's emotional engagement with the story. Think of this process of rising conflict like building up a raging fire. You don't wait until one log burns out to toss the next one on. The more fuel you add and the more regularly you add it, the brighter the fire burns.

Ideally, through her interaction with the supporting character, the protagonist becomes conscious little by little of her blind spot—a weakness that reveals itself to her over the course of the story. In this way, we might say that an insanely great supporting character brings healing to the protagonist, and vice-versa. Through their differences, iron sharpens iron. The protagonist and supporting character challenge each other in new and unanticipated ways. Sometimes, the protagonist resists change and pushes back so forcefully that the supporting character has enough and walks away. When that's the case, a large part of Act Three focuses on winning back the love-interest or friend.

I think you're ready to start brainstorming what this relationship looks like for the protagonist in your story.

◆ Exercise 10. *By now you've read up to page 40 of the script you selected. That means you've encountered the main supporting character. If you're reading a romantic comedy, chances are you met this character before page 10 or at least by the inciting incident. (This is what is known as the "meet cute.")*

1. Who is the main supporting character in the movie you are reading? Why does the protagonist meet this character?

2. Describe the scene when the encounter takes place. What is the setup? How does the protagonist react? What is the supporting character's reaction to the protagonist?
3. How does the writer make us understand from the outset that the supporting character is in some key way different from the protagonist?
4. Does the supporting character highlight a weakness of the protagonist? If so, why and how?

◆ Exercise 11. *Think about your supporting character.*

1. How is the supporting character different from the protagonist?
2. In what ways might such a difference manifest itself through action and the way the supporting character interacts with the protagonist?
3. Does the supporting character recognize the protagonist's weakness right away or will that weakness be discovered over time?
4. In the course of that journey, what will the supporting character also discover about himself?
5. Why is the protagonist the only person in the world who might bring about this change in the supporting character?
6. Reading assignment. For tomorrow, read on to page 60 in the script you're studying. Take time to make notes about the interaction between the protagonist and supporting character. How does the writer convey their similarities and differences through action? Record two or three specific examples of how the supporting character introduces a new or heightened dimension of conflict.

STEP 8. THE MIDPOINT

The tide turns.

I think the midpoint is one of the most interesting points in story design. As the tent-pole at the center of the narrative, it holds everything together. At the midpoint, the stakes are raised once again, although at first this may not be glaringly obvious. In no small part, this is where the protagonist makes a decisive move from passive to active. We've seen how, at the end of Act One, the protagonist cannot simply be swept away by the events and carried over into Act Two. That said, this does not imply that the protagonist actively drives the direction of the plot at the end of Act One. Rather, she proactively responds to the adventure into which she has been invited. At the midpoint, the protagonist is no longer content with responding to the circumstances around her and makes an active decision that in turn changes the direction of the plot.

Let's consider an example from classical theatre: Shakespeare's MACBETH. The play has benefited from several good film adaptations. I'm a fan of the 2006 version created for PBS and starring Patrick Stewart. (Be sure to take a look at a printed copy of the play as well, since movie adaptations tend to cut and shift scenes around.)

In the first scene of MACBETH, we come face to face with three witch-like creatures, perhaps a hat-tip to the ancient world's Fates. They meet on a heath in Scotland. We know from the dialogue that things are not as they appear: "Fair is foul and foul is fair." The witches are up to something. They reappear a few scenes later to announce to Macbeth that he will be named Thayne of Cawdor and then king. At this point, we are well prepared to mistrust them. (The witches also foretell of Macbeth's best friend, Banquo, becoming father to a line of kings.) As if to corroborate the witches' report, a messenger arrives straight from King Duncan, announcing that Macbeth has been elevated to the rank of Thayne of Cawdor. What foul play is afoot?

Macbeth and Banquo may have thought little of the ill-wrought prophecy, had the messenger not appeared. Yet, once they learn of Macbeth's new title, they cannot keep from wondering. What if the witches' prophecy is true? Will Macbeth be king? The treachery is set in motion. We witness, from the audience's ranks, the very first moment of the hatching of Macbeth's diabolical plan. He'll now take matters into his own hands, murder the king and bring about the fulfillment of the prophecy himself. To what ends man will succumb in order to advance himself! (Little has changed.)

To set his plan in motion, Macbeth writes to his wife. We join Lady Macbeth as she reads the letter. We cannot help but be filled with unease when she complies all too willingly with the preparations. Duncan's days are numbered. Yet, Macbeth arrives home with a changed mind. Duncan has shown him favor; he cannot murder his king! In a terrifying scene, Lady Macbeth holds her husband to the murder plan; he succumbs to the pressure.

In terms of story design, Lady Macbeth functions as Christopher Vogler's "threshold guardian," who gives her husband the nudge he needs to cross over into Act Two. However, by the time we reach the play's midpoint, things have changed. We witness Macbeth single-handedly plot the murder of his best friend, Banquo. When Lady Macbeth asks what her husband is up to, he avoids revealing the plan to her altogether, preferring to meet privately with the henchmen and have Banquo's murder carried out in secret. Macbeth's move from passive to active shifts the course of the story and seals Macbeth's downward spiral into self-destruction. There can be no turning back.

Modern movies and novels aren't the first storytelling media to focus on the midpoint as a moment of decisive shifting. It so happens that the authors of twelfth-century narratives, including the earliest Arthurian legends, were careful to place an important revelation at the midpoint of their tales. It's right in the middle, for example, that Chrétien de Troyes reveals the true name of the anonymous *Knight of the Cart* (ca. 1170), dividing the book into two neatly organized halves. Lancelot's true identity is revealed in the battle sequence right at the center. He takes a stand.

GLADIATOR employs a similar technique. Maximus's identity is revealed to Commodus at the midpoint. The notorious "Spaniard" turns his back to the emperor, a breathtaking act of defiance. Then, under duress, he removes his helmet and reveals his true identity, precipitating a decisive turn in the story. Maximus no longer benefits from the safety of anonymity. Commodus knows his greatest enemy lives.

The midpoint shoots the plot off in a new direction, from which there's no turning back. It signals the beginning of the downward spiral of the second half of Act Two, and the protagonist must now confront obstacles of increasingly monumental proportion. Macbeth's victory is a false high; the success of the murder plan is the beginning of the end for him. It precipitates his ruin. In contrast, Maximus's public revelation is a false low; while it ought to precipitate his ruin, it sets in motion the events that allow him to fulfill his promise to Marcus Aurelius and give Rome back to the people. This rule of thumb is typical of the midpoint in blockbuster movies today. (You can read further about highs and lows in Blake Snyder's *Save the Cat* and Robert McKee's *Story*.)

At the threshold to Act Two, the protagonist could conceivably blame either the circumstances into which she has been thrust, or even the threshold guardian, for motivating her to make a decisive commitment to crossing into the extraordinary world. At the midpoint, the protagonist becomes fully responsible for the course the story takes. Sooner or later, she will face the consequences of those actions.

◆ Exercise 12. *Let's recap and take another look at the script you're reading.*

1. What happens at the midpoint? How does this create a major turning point and precipitate a shift in the direction of the story?
2. How does the writer set up the midpoint? How many adventures take place in the first half of Act Two?
3. Consider two or three of your favorite movies. How does the protagonist move from passive to active at the midpoint?

STEP 9. ALL DOWNHILL

Everything goes from bad to worse.

In the second half of Shakespeare's MACBETH, the protagonist's world spins out of control. Macbeth sees Banquo's ghost during the banquet celebrating his coronation as king. The murder he planned and the haunting memory of betraying his friend precipitate Macbeth's downward spiral into madness. Lady Macbeth can no longer live with her own guilt, nor with her husband's demise. She takes her own life—but it's a matter of time until the treachery of Duncan's murder is revealed and the Scottish nobles settle the score.

I find it helpful to think of the difference between the first and second halves of Act Two in terms of the values in conflict. The first half of Act Two privileges the protagonist's values. In the second half, antagonism escalates. At the end of Act One, the protagonist commits to championing a certain worldview—most commonly the underdog values, which stand in opposition to the dominant values of the surrounding external world.

For example, in C.S. Lewis's classic, THE LION, THE WITCH AND THE WARDROBE (adapted for the big screen in 2005), the children vow to fight for Aslan, justice, and the return of good to Narnia. The evil and tyrannical White Witch has quashed happiness, hope, and even Christmas. The values championed by the White Witch and her cronies dominate, along with everything that comes along with such a worldview—oppression, tyranny, fear, evil, grief, despair. To restore the rightful order, the witch must be defeated, along with the values for which she stands.

During the first half of Act Two, the protagonist has made measurable strides towards achieving her goal. In turn, this motivates the antagonist to push back, creating a rising conflict. The shift occurs at the midpoint—it's all downhill from here. Think of it as a game of thrust and parry. The protagonist fights back, but the antagonist pushes back even stronger, forming a chain of action and reaction. When one character makes a move, the other responds. No matter how strongly the protagonist counters, the antagonist gains ground. At their very core, great stories are driven by conflict.

For the conflict to be palpable, the antagonist must present a real threat and be at least as strong as the protagonist until the very end. (Robert McKee calls this the "principle of antagonism.") At the beginning of many great stories, the antagonist—Darth Vader, the White Witch, the Green Goblin—is stronger than the protagonist—Luke Skywalker, the Pevensie children, Spider-man. But if you set your protagonist-antagonist relationship up well, the audience will sense that the protagonist has the potential to grow and we hope that she'll grow along the character arc enough to become capable of overthrowing her adversary. The story chronicles this growth process, or character arc. In ROGUE ONE: A STAR WARS STORY (2016), Jyn spends a good part of the movie not wanting to get involved with the rebellion. However, when she finds her father, and he dies in her arms, she vows to complete the mission. Thanks to her leadership, a group of rebels (who go rogue against the decision of the council) seek out the Death Star plans and beam them up to a cruiser and to Princess Leia. Over the course of the film, as she overcomes adversity and faces off against the antagonist, Jyn evolves into a courageous fighter, who not only takes a stand against the Empire, but is willing to lay down her life in the sacrifice of her higher calling.

Long ago, Aristotle discussed this process of actualization in his philosophical treatise, *Metaphysics*. The character arc is not just about the self-realization of the protagonist and becoming who she wants to be. Rather, it's about accepting and even embracing that calling for which she has been placed in this world. The calling is out there. It's greater than the protagonist. That's what Joseph Campbell means when he talks about the "call to greatness."

As the protagonist explores and grows in the first half of Act Two, we gain a firm sense of her raw potential to overthrow the enemy. As THE MATRIX (1999) puts it, the protagonist is "the one" upon whom rests all hope. This principle equally applies to sports movies and romantic comedies. The protagonist might be the only person who can lead the team to victory, or the made-in-heaven love match, or, for that matter, the worst imaginable love match who turns out to be surprisingly ideal. WONDER WOMAN (2017) marks the transition from passive to active by showing Diana Prince follow Steve and his friends to the front, and specifically, to No Man's Land, the mile-long stretch where no man can cross. It's here that she decides to take her stand. Diana throws off her cloak, reveals her armor and equipment, and sets across the forbidden stretch, deflecting bullets and missiles as she runs, faster and faster, towards the enemy line. Her true identity comes to life on screen, not only for the audience, but also for the characters in the story book world.

And yet, it's important to remember the antagonist cannot roll over and admit defeat. He's a force to be reckoned with, or there would be no story. In most cases, the antagonist wants precisely the same thing as the protagonist: the MacGuffin. But he plans on putting it to very different use, motivated by his own worldview and set of beliefs. Keep in mind these beliefs are real, logical, and even (as far as the antagonist is concerned) correct. Antagonists only seem crazy to us in so far as their way of doing life and business (or even love) stands in direct opposition to our worldview. But to them, it's utterly logical. Think about Hannibal Lecter in SILENCE OF THE LAMBS (1991) and you'll see what I mean. The antagonist is also most likely committed to winning the protagonist over to his own side. We see this, for example, in STAR WARS V: THE EMPIRE STRIKES BACK (1980), when Darth Vader beckons Luke to join the dark side. The converse is equally true. Oftentimes, the protagonist will try her utmost to win the antagonist over to the light. If the adversary cannot be converted, ultimately, he must be eliminated.

As things spiral downhill and out of control, the second half of Act

Two ushers in the rule of the dominant values of the story book world. Throughout this attack sequence, the protagonist must confront—and risk defeat by—a series of ever more challenging obstacles. Thus, by the time we reach the end of Act Two, about seventy percent of the way through the story, things have gotten so bad that the protagonist finds her back against the wall. She may even be tempted, at that point, to give up. Perhaps the love interest is lost, or the antagonist has killed someone dear to the protagonist, like a mentor figure. Perhaps, even, the best player on the team has been disqualified and the final match seems doomed. For all intents and purposes, we've hit a brick wall. In many stories, this is a good time for the supporting character to step in and offer a pep talk or fresh perspective.

I love how GRAVITY (2013) achieves the brick wall. Sandra Bullock's character, Ryan, loses all hope and turns off her air supply. Her colleague, Matt (played by George Clooney), shows up to try and talk her back. We are incredulous. How could Matt have survived that space walk without air? Once his pep talk is over, all becomes clear. We realize Ryan has hallucinated. Nonetheless, it's exactly what she needs to push through the wall and attempt the flight home, armed with a renewed sense of purpose and reason to live.

This is an important aspect of the second half of Act Two. To end the attack sequence and make the final transition into Act Three, the protagonist must achieve a moment of self-realization. It can be as simple as Jack Nicholson's character, Melvin, looking out the window in the rain in AS GOOD AS IT GETS (1997) with the sudden realization that he cannot live without Helen. (Winning back his love interest then becomes the object of Act Three.) In GLADIATOR, Lucilla reminds Maximus of her father's dream for Rome. Although Maximus rejects her supplication to rise up against Commodus with the army and Senate behind him, Lucilla's words strike a nerve. Maximus's self-realization breaks down the wall and ushers in Act Three—the quest to give Rome back to the people. The protagonist's ultimate transformation is so inspiring that even the jaded Proximo becomes an ally in the quest for freedom.

Blake Snyder calls this moment the "All Is Lost." I prefer to see the brick wall as the final, most decisive threshold the protagonist crosses in her journey. The test readies her to confront the antagonist, face to face, in the final climax of Act Three. Without this critical moment of commitment—which mirrors and magnifies the commitment at the end of Act One—the transition to Act Three will inevitably fail. In other words, the brick wall echoes and amplifies the kind of dilemma the protagonist confronted around page seventeen. This is the moment of final choosing. This is the ultimate commitment to the quest. Earlier, she didn't completely realize what she was getting into. Now, however, she makes an informed decision; she understands she cannot turn back. Life will never be as it was before. The only path is through. She grabs the metaphorical sledge hammer and smashes the wall down. That's the stuff of which great final act breaks are made.

Throughout this book, I focus on stories in which the protagonist wins out in the end. If, however, your antagonist wins, practice suggests that successful plays and movies tend to reverse the sequence. At the midpoint, things turn for the better for the protagonist. By the end of Act Two, the protagonist is at an all-time high, instead of the brick wall. The rule of thumb is simple. Wherever the protagonist finds herself at the end of Act Three (defeat or triumph), she finds herself in the opposite position at the end of Act Two. (In the case of a romantic comedy, keep in mind the antagonist is typically the love-interest.)

Before turning you over to some more exercises, I want to draw your attention to an important question: Why is it so hard for the protagonist to dig deep down inside and summon the strength it takes to push through the brick wall? This goes back, once again, to the character arc. Remember that blind spot only the supporting character can see? In spite of all the growth the protagonist has accomplished during the journey, she has not yet healed that character flaw or inner hurt. Until she transcends it, victory will escape her. That's why so often near the end of Act Two the supporting character gives the protagonist a pep talk. She might not want to hear it—she might even send the supporting character packing. But ultimately, the truth communicated to the protagonist will force her to confront reality and change. Over the course of their relationship, the supporting character has earned the trust of the protagonist (and vice versa), which weighs heavily with the protagonist. It could be, however, that the protagonist is at such an all-time psychological low at the end of Act Two that she breaks that trust or betrays the friendship. Whatever the case may be, here, at the brick wall, the protagonist can no longer turn a blind eye to her need. Once that need is made clear, through whatever means necessary, she has only two choices—change, or abandon the quest.

The decision the protagonist makes to pro-actively deal with her need, and the process of beginning to heal, completes her growth cycle. Now, and not one moment before, she is ready for the final face-off against the antagonist. Now, she knows who she is and what she stands for. She understands her role within a bigger picture. The commitment to follow through against all odds, and face her innermost fears, marks the transition into Act Three. There can be no more hesitation.

◆ Exercise 13. *Let's take another look at the script you're reading. Continue to the end of Act Two, probably around page 70 or 80, depending on the total length of the script.*

1. Which values dominate during the first half of Act Two? Describe two or three events that clearly show these values in action.
2. At what point in the story does the apparent progress of the underdog values shift to the attack of the dominant values? How is the shift set up? To what event must the protagonist react?
3. Who is the antagonist in the script? What drives and motivates him? Why?
4. Describe at least two specific moments when the antagonist's desire enters into conflict with what the

Basics of Story Design

protagonist wants. Why do we care whether or not the protagonist defeats the forces of antagonism?

◆ Exercise 14. *Now, let's think about your own story.*

1. What is most dear to your protagonist? Why?
2. How will the antagonist directly oppose what the protagonist wants? Brainstorm two or three ways in which the antagonist will pose an obstacle to the protagonist.

◆ Exercise 15. *Let's go back to the script you're reading and dig further in to the second half of Act Two.*

1. Pick out two or three major setbacks that challenge the protagonist in the second half of Act Two.
2. How does the antagonist set these in motion?
3. How does the protagonist break through temporary defeat at the end of Act Two and commit to finishing the journey?

STEP 10. THE GRAND FINALE

We're here, at the end of the journey... almost.

Act Three should be the most fast-paced, end-game-driven act of the movie. It's time to wrap up all the story lines, carry the jeopardy through to the highest point, and place the protagonist in such circumstances that she will now square off, once and for all, against the dominant values and forces of antagonism. Wrapping up need not entail tying up everything into a neat little package with a bow on top. My point in this chapter isn't to exhaust what it takes to create a great ending. For now, I want you to know enough to begin mapping out your plot.

Every great ending has a beginning, middle, and end. We'll explore what this looks like through some examples.

In STAR WARS IV: A NEW HOPE, the three-part ending can be summarized in the most barebones format as follows: First, Luke and the rebellion articulate the plan. A weakness has been found in the Death Star. It's a long shot, but one proton torpedo fired in the right spot will blow up the whole thing. The rebels have a plan, but jeopardy remains high. Only a perfectly aimed shot stands between them and oblivion. Can the targeting computer even make that shot? We must sense that the protagonist is up against overbearing odds. At most, there's a glimmer of the hope of success. The final battle surpasses all other moments of testing the protagonist has faced over the course of the story.

Second, Luke and the X-wing team make their approach. The ticking clock counts down—very literally, on screen—as the rebel base approaches firing range. As X-wing pilots get picked off one by one, the towers stop firing and one fighter even gets a shot at the target…but misses the mark. We are now in the middle of the end, mirroring the downhill spiral of the second half of Act Two. Darth Vader decides to settle the score once and for all. The pilots are trapped, sitting ducks, until only Luke remains. This part of Act Three mimics, to all intents and purposes, the brick wall. Except now, Luke has no choice to make: he pushes on. He already committed to carrying the mission to term when he passed into Act Three. His conviction is palpable.

Isolated from everyone else, Luke makes the final attempt. Note how jeopardy continues to carry the scene. Darth Vader even gets a lock on Luke. In an unexpected reversal, Han Solo returns, fires Vader off into space, and Luke makes the shot in the nick of time. As we cheer along with the characters, there's only one matter of business remaining—one last scene of resolution to show the results of the final face-off, or climax. The crisis has, for now, been averted.

Even the protagonist of a romantic comedy has a plan going into a great third act, an idea on how to get the girl (or guy). This last-ditch effort may fall short. Maybe the love interest wasn't at the airport or the plane already left, or perhaps the protagonist can't make it to city hall in time to halt the wedding. Ultimately, though, a new piece of information alerts the lover that things are not as they first appear. There's still a chance to win the heart of the love interest but it will take making a grand stand. The affection-averse title character of **JERRY MAGUIRE** (1996) must confess his love publicly in front of all of Dorothy's friends. In **NOTTING HILL**, William summons the courage to speak out in front of every reporter in London. And in **ABOUT TIME**, a son spends the very last of his extra time in the best way he can imagine—by taking a walk with his father. In this last example, the grand stand may be private but it is one nonetheless, for the protagonist finds truth and beauty in the simple things of life we all have the tendency to take for granted.

GLADIATOR, too, offers up a great three-part finale. Maximus commits to meeting his garrison outside the city and makes considerable progress toward that goal, only to find out that Cicero is tied to his horse and Commodus has found him out. As we approach the final climax, the stakes are raised even further when Commodus and Maximus privately face off beneath the Coliseum; Maximus in shackles, Commodus resplendent in white robes and shiny battle armor. Everything about this moment portrays Commodus as the dominant figure. The antagonist is on the verge of triumph. As extra insurance, he fatally wounds Maximus before facing him in the arena. (In order for it to be believable that Commodus could actually face off against Maximus, the writers carefully illustrated his gift in swordsmanship during a practice scene earlier in the script.)

The end of the end—the final face-off, the climax of the movie—is the physical fight in front of all of Rome. The unexpected reversal comes in the form of Maximus's former friend in the legion, now of the imperial guard, who refuses to furnish the emperor a replacement sword. Maximus may die, but he overcomes every possible obstacle to give Rome back to the people before joining his family in the afterlife. (The actions of the legionary friend—his refusal to yield a sword to Commodus—echo Han Solo's surprise return. Writers often refer to such moments as the *Judas reversal* or *Han Solo moment*.)

Watch as many movies as you can, read scripts, plays and great novels and ask yourself: What is it about this story that commands staying power, year after year, century after century? Undoubtedly, you'll find a great plot, great characters, unexpected twists and turns. You'll identify a great ending that carries jeopardy right through the whole of Act Three. At the end of the day, when the credits roll, that's what will be on the minds of the audience as they walk away. This is the grand finale. This is where the rubber finally meets the road. Make it count. This is when the protagonist, armed with everything she has learned, solidifies her ultimate transformation and faces off against the forces of antagonism for the final stand. The fate of the world—the love story, or perhaps the survival of the family, or even the human race—hangs in the balance. The protagonist's fate is sealed, and in that moment, so, too, is the undergirding premise of the movie.

Great stories don't end in stalemate. At high noon, one cowboy makes the shot; only one walks away alive.

♦ Exercise 16. *Our exercises in this chapter focus on the climax. Finish the script you selected and answer the following questions:*

1. Describe the final climax scene. How does it begin? What is the middle of the end? How does it resolve?
2. Let's take a closer look at how we arrive at the climax. What are the major events that take place prior to the final face-off? And how does the writer keep jeopardy at an all-time high moving towards the climax?
3. What's the protagonist's ultimate commitment crossing the threshold into Act Three? How does the writer make it difficult for the protagonist to reach that goal?

♦ Exercise 17. *Now, let's turn to the story you're designing.*

1. We'll begin with the climax itself. What will be the jeopardy in the final scene?
2. Brainstorm at least three ways to make the confrontation original. How might you vary the setting or defy the audience's expectations?
3. Great climax scenes often contain an element of surprise, or reversal. Right when the going gets tough, an unexpected twist enables the protagonist to pull through (think Han Solo's return in STAR WARS IV: A NEW HOPE). Brainstorm one or two possible reversals that would increase the suspense during your final face-off.
4. Thinking backwards now to the act break, what commitment will your protagonist make at the end of Act Two and why?
5. Keeping in mind that act of commitment, how can you stack the deck against the protagonist so that she has to overcome almost insurmountable adversity to defeat the antagonist?
6. Finally, brainstorm at least two possibilities for the

resolution scene. Take into consideration your opening image. How will your resolution reflect the transformation of the protagonist and the effect on the world around her?

STEP 11. BUILDING BLOCKS

By now, you have a general idea of your story.

Bravo! You've read through an entire script, too. It's time to solidify the major building blocks of your story. Completing a story design worksheet is your task for today. You've already brainstormed most of the building blocks in previous chapters, so now the object is to bring them all together, in the same document. This is also a good time to decide if you'd like to make changes and adjustments. Great writers rarely settle for their initial idea.

If you hop on over to basicsofstorydesign.com, you can download some helpful worksheets and visual tools to assist you in this process.

I also encourage you to check out other overviews and explanations, like Blake Snyder's beat sheet in *Save the Cat*. While most writers engage similar building blocks in the crafting of their stories, the explanations they provide for them are different. We all tend to agree on several key elements, but you'll see, for example, that I sometimes have one (the brick wall) where Blake has three ("all is lost," "dark night of the soul," and "break into three"). I've found this unified approach to a single building block, or "beat," at the end of Act Two provides me with a more punchy transition into Act Three. However, you may prefer a lengthier transition. It's up to you to decide what works best for your story.

I'm also grateful to teachers at UCLA for helping me see the true value of the *character moments* I've included in my own outlining process. These play such a key role for me in shaping the first and second halves of Act Two. Making these kinds of moments count is a great way to keep the character arc on track and ensure your character is growing as the story progresses. I can't recommend them enough.

The verdict? To each his (or her) own. There's no single, correct way to achieve the structural integrity of a story. One person's process doesn't eclipse or render obsolete other approaches. It's really a question of finding out what works for you, and covers all of the highs and lows discussed in steps 1-10. Some writers may prefer to get everything down on paper, driven by inspiration alone. That's fine. I'd argue that at some point, if you want to have a chance of selling your screenplay or seeing it made into a movie, you're going to have to integrate each of the building blocks and take your pages back down to outline to find out what's working—and what's not. Learn structure so that, ultimately, you can forget about it and embrace it as a natural part of your visual storytelling tool kit.

At the end of the day, it's up to you to find your voice and develop your own method. Draw upon my experience and that of others, and you'll eventually come up with your own outlining principles. Make your story, and your process, your own.

- ♦ Exercise 18. *Fill out your story worksheet. For convenience, I've included a review of each of the main building blocks and their reason for being below, along with approximate page references for a 100-page spec script.*

  - ○ **Point of Attack (pp. 1-2, at most 1-3).** This is the beginning of your movie. You'll want to try a few options in order to pick a scene that best introduces the premise and themes. Remember to showcase the values at stake in the story world. If need be, go back to Lajos Egri and study the art of the dramatic premise.

  - ○ **The World as We Know It, or the Ordinary World.** It's time to build a **sequence** (a series of scenes) to introduce

Basics of Story Design

the reader and audience to your protagonist. Remember: *Show, don't tell.* Actions and interactions are more powerful than background and exposition.

- As part of the **ordinary world**, you'll want to signal that **a storm is brewing.** Things may appear to be continuing on as usual, but you want to create the impression that the protagonist's world (and life) is on the brink of a change. Things cannot continue as they are. You're setting up the opportunity for an event to take place that invites the protagonist into a new journey.

- **Inciting Incident, or Catalyst (pp. 10-12).** One day, everything changes. Remember, we're just lighting the fuse here. The stick of dynamite doesn't explode quite yet. This is the day everything changes, even if the protagonist is unaware of how much that change will impact her life. As far as the protagonist is concerned, this isn't necessarily her business; she can still avoid or turn down the invitation. Great writers have different names for this story moment, but you can be sure that their stories all have one.

- **Dilemma (p. 17).** By page 17 at the latest, you want to up the ante. The stick of dynamite explodes and the protagonist faces a decision: to stay home, or follow the invitation into a new world. It's not clear yet as to what decision the protagonist will make. Something's going to have to happen to cause her to jump off the ledge. And when she does, she won't fully understand what she's getting herself into. Around the dilemma point, we get an initial sense that the character may be on the brink of biting off more than she can chew.

- **Protagonist commits to crossing the threshold (pp. 25-27).** It's time to commit to the quest. Reread Christopher

Vogler's *Writer's Journey* if you need a refresher on this important story moment. Something happens and prompts the protagonist to make a proactive decision to move forward. Remember, the protagonist cannot simply be swept along into the action. An active decision must be made and clearly presented in the story. The protagonist must take ownership of this moment. She has agency. Moreover, I like to keep in mind that this commitment sheds light on the dramatic premise. The protagonist makes a decision to take a stand, through action, for something she believes in. Typically, her position is to become a champion of the underdog values of the story world, or at the very least, to align with them and be willing to take a step towards championing them.

[End of Act One]

- **Adventure Sequence.** We're in the **extraordinary world** and it's time to engage in the **adventure**. Remember, you don't want to up the stakes again until the midpoint. This is your opportunity to present us with the rules of the new world, and stage events that challenge your protagonist to grow along the character arc. Each event in the adventure is an opportunity for your main character to grow and build confidence.

- **Gaining Support (p. 30).** Don't forget to introduce your supporting character. The main purpose of the supporting character is to present a new influence for the protagonist. Interacting with this character will help your protagonist grow through the character arc. In a 100-page script, you want this introduction to happen no later than page 30 or 35. Ideally, you'll weave the path and desire line of the supporting character directly into the protagonist's story and desire line. For example in STAR WARS IV: A NEW

HOPE, Han's path intersects with Luke and Obi-Wan because there's a price on his head, and he needs the money. Although Luke and Han don't share the same desire line, their individual MacGuffins temporarily align in the same direction. In other words, Han embraces a shared goal, but he pursues that goal for different underlying philosophical principles and motivations than those that drive Luke and Obi-Wan. (Ultimately, when their paths bifurcate, and no longer align, Han will leave Luke and set off to settle his debt. But he, too, will have grown over the course of the story. That's why he comes back: supporting his friend and fighting for something greater than himself has overtaken his desire to settle the price on his head.)

- **The Adventure Sequence Continues.** With the supporting character in tow, the protagonist continues to progress towards the critical midpoint and live the adventure of the extraordinary world.

When it comes to executing the whole Adventure Sequence, I find it especially useful to build a series of three or four mini-goals to help me get from the threshold crossing all the way to the midpoint. For example, let's say our overarching goal is to "deliver the plans to Alderaan." (Sound familiar? Good.) Then I'm going to think of three mini-goals upon which my protagonist can realistically focus in order to get them all the way to the midpoint. (1) We need to get into the city and find a pilot. (2) We have to make sure we don't draw the attention of the Empire. (3) We have to get to the ship and make the leap to hyperspace.

Then, it's a question of designing scenes that make it difficult for the protagonist to achieve each of these goals. First, to get into the city, we have to get past the stormtroopers. Luke and Obi-Wan succeed in the famous "these are not the droids you're looking for" scene. This is an important moment for Luke, because it showcases Obi-Wan's Jedi powers in action. It makes him a believer in the Force. Second, as much as Luke tries to fly under the radar in the space tavern, he gets involved in a brawl. This forces Obi-Wan to show his hand and blow their disguise when he pulls out his lightsaber in Luke's defense. Enter mini-goal three. Obi-Wan has found a pilot, but Luke finds Han's attitude off-putting. However, the ticking clock set in motion by the brawl has drawn the attention of some stormtroopers. There's no time to lose. The race is on to get back to the ship, under attack and enemy fire. The ship takes off and (after a minor hiccup) makes the leap to hyperspace. The adventure sequence is a resounding success! Except… there's no Alderaan.

o **Character Moment #1 (around p. 40).** The protagonist does something she wouldn't have done in Act One, based on what she has learned and most likely the influence exerted by the supporting character. This demonstrates through action that your protagonist is evolving through the character arc.

o **Midpoint (p. 50). The tide turns**. If the movie is to end with the triumph of the underdog values, the midpoint represents a setback. Most importantly, the protagonist moves from **passive to active**. This decision changes the course of the story and is a direct cause of the **brick wall**—although the protagonist doesn't know that yet.

[End of Act Two, First Half]

o **All Downhill: Attack of the Dominant Values.** Everything goes from bad to worse. The second half of Act Two represents a series of ever-increasing setbacks for the protagonist. Keep in mind that, for me, it's not as simple as the "bad guys closing in," as Blake Snyder puts it. Rather, the shift from passive to active that the protagonist made at the midpoint has likely led her to do something that was premature, or a little too bold. At the midpoint, by taking a stand and shifting the direction of the story, the protagonist pushes the plot in a direction that now causes harm to those on the journey with her. Unknowingly, she oftentimes transfers the strategic advantage to the antagonist.

In keeping with my approach to outlining the first half of Act One, I like to split this second half of Act Two into three or four mini-goals and adventures, to make the progression specific. The only difference is that this time, the forces of antagonism have the upper hand at every step of the way.

Taking once again STAR WARS IV: A NEW HOPE as our model (but you'll be able to do this with any carefully constructed story), Luke moves from passive to active when he realizes the Princess is detained in the cell block. Note how Han resists, siding with Obi-Wan for the first time in the movie: even the old man told them to stay put. (1) We've got to get into the cellblock and find the princess; (2) We've got to get out of the cellblock; (3) We have to rendezvous with Obi-Wan and escape. (By this time, he'll have the shield down.) At each step of the way, the adventure goes from bad to worse. The plan to get into the cell block ultimately succeeds, but as Princess Leia herself points out, they have no plan for getting back out, and are now under enemy fire. (2) She takes matters into her own hands and blows them an escape route... straight into the garbage compactor. There, they confront the octopus-like creature that attacks Luke, and when it leaves, the walls start moving in. C-3PO saves the day, but (3) when they attempt to rejoin Obi-Wan (who did get the shield down), he faces off against Darth Vader and sacrifices himself so they can escape. Things are looking pretty bad for the rebels. The princess even suspects their enemies allowed them to escape and that there's a tracking device on board.

- **Character Moment #2 (around pp. 60-65).** The protagonist does something she wouldn't and couldn't have done in the first half of Act Two. This moment represents a step further along the character arc than the first character moment.

- **The Brick Wall (p. 70).** Blake Snyder, in *Save the Cat*, likes to think of this point as the "all is lost." Indeed, the brick wall represents the ultimate low for the protagonist. But more importantly, I like to remember that the protagonist now faces a decision that amplifies the commitment she made to the quest at the end of Act One. It's time to pick up the sledgehammer, break through the wall, and **recommit to the quest**. Oftentimes, the quest is redefined and a bigger picture comes into focus. The protagonist is ready to enter Act Three. (You'll note that I choose not to separate this moment from the act break. I find the story is more powerful when the two are conflated.)

[End of Act Two, Second Half]

- **The Final Face-Off (around pp. 95-98).** Act Three is defined by three major movements: (1) The beginning of the end—the protagonist commits to a plan, mimicking the crossing of the threshold in Act One. (2) The middle of the end—the plan seems to work but then experiences major push-back, leading to the impression that the protagonist has reached the end of the road. This segment mimics the upwards and downwards movements of the first and second halves of Act Two. (3) The protagonist now makes a bold move to confront the antagonist in the final face-off. Conflict is at an all-time high and culminates in the **climax** of the movie. (This is the moment that, for Aristotle, provokes *catharsis* in the audience.)

- **Resolution (pp. 99-100).** We turn the cameras off after a meaningful scene that shows us how the ordinary world has changed as a result of the events portrayed in the movie. This is the **new world** and **new equilibrium**. We experience, first-hand, the results of the protagonist's quest and inner transformation on the story world.

[End of Act Three]

STEP 12. BACK TO BASICS

Congratulations, you have an outline!

Not satisfied? Don't worry. You'll have plenty of time to improve on the basic building blocks you articulated yesterday. While it might be tempting to move straight on to *step outline* (we'll talk more about that in the coming days), I want us to pause and think of ways to elevate your story. There are countless ways your outline can be made better at this point in the game—and if you work on eliminating problems now, or making it stronger, you'll save a great deal of time later. Remember the golden rule: All good writing is rewriting. And in this case, great story design is redesign, tweaking, and trying out other possibilities. (The team at Work & Co, a design company based in Brooklyn, once told me they went through close to two thousand iterations and tweaks before finalizing their famous redesign of the Virgin America website in 2014. I want you to think of your screenplay as a product, and I want you to give that product design as much attention as it deserves and requires to see the light of day and be marketable, so that it gets made into a movie, reaches the public, and achieves box office success.)

In order to be highly marketable, your story needs to be based on a big idea that is unique, appeals to a wide audience, and can be distilled down to a single *logline* that allows you to picture the whole movie.

Chances are, at this point, your story—and even your big idea—is too complex. Let's work on refining them. Think about how to reduce your outline down to a simple, elegant structure. The more simple the backbone, the better the story. And the easier it will be for you to keep it on spine. If you're dissatisfied with the building blocks you prepared yesterday, this is a great opportunity to rethink them before you get further invested. Keep in mind that it's absolutely fine to throw them away and start with something new if a unique, appealing and simple idea emerges over the course of your work today. Too many people worry about troubleshooting when the script is completely drafted. By then, you're so emotionally invested in the project after hours and hours of work—possibly spread over years—you cannot see the forest for the trees. Today, we're going to play around with your concept and decide if you want to refine it, revise it, or throw it out in favor of something better.

First, let's discuss how you go about constructing your logline. The logline is a brief summary of your movie. It should be evocative. After reading the logline, a reader or producer should be able to envision the plot of the whole movie. It should also be simple and focus on the protagonist. You'll want to indicate what the protagonist is seeking to accomplish and the struggles she must face to get there. There's no cookie-cutter format your logline needs to follow, as long as all the aforementioned elements are present—all of this in a single sentence (or two at the most). For example, a possible logline for FINDING NEMO might be: "When his son is kidnapped, Marlin, an anxious clownfish, struggles to overcome his fear of the unknown and braves the wide ocean and all its dangers to rescue him."

◆ Exercise 19. *It's your turn.*

1. *Write your logline!* Don't worry if you have to try on a few for size.
2. Perhaps your concept seems boring or trivial. Maybe it's just too similar to other movies. To get a boost of creativity, turn it into an animated movie. Or, if you were planning on writing an animated movie, turn it into a live-action story. Switching genres works wonders for the imagination, even if you revert back to your original idea. *Now, write the new logline.*

♦   Exercise 20. *Switch some other elements around.*

> 1. What happens if you change the protagonist's gender, or occupation? How can you make the character less predictable?
> 2. Try playing with the context or setting. Instead of your story taking place in a school, what would happen if you moved it to a police station? Or a Marine training camp? What about a meals-on-wheels program? Have some fun with this.
> 3. There's nothing like taking a journey through time and space to get those creative juices flowing. Change your movie into science fiction. Set it in the future, or in an alternate past —perhaps, even, in a different world altogether.
> 4. Now, give your main character a strange tick. Think of Dory in FINDING NEMO, who suffers from short-term memory loss. Or Olaf in FROZEN, the snowman who dreams of summer. How does this spice up your story?

You get the idea. There are as many combinations as you're willing to explore. This is one of the truly fun things about writing. Andrew Stanton (FINDING NEMO) could have written a story about a human father who loses his son on the playground outside his apartment. Perhaps, even, that father lost his wife five years earlier in a tragic accident. Maybe his son gets abducted from the playground by the mafia as an act of retaliation because the father is an attorney who just sentenced a major crime boss to prison...the possibilities are endless. Instead, Stanton opted for a fish and opened up an opportunity to explore the marvels of life under the ocean. What if Marlin and Nemo had been chimps? What if they were starfish? See what I mean?

Now that you've settled on a logline draft, it's always a good idea to return to some character basics, too.

When asked what convinces him to say *yes* to a project, Robert

Duvall told a packed ballroom at South by Southwest Film in 2014: "The character." It's that simple. When it comes to great movies, he added, "The pickings get a little bit scarce." And when it comes to great movies with insanely great characters, the options are even scarcer.

Michael Arndt told me something similar a few years earlier: There's no market for a bad script, but great scripts are in high demand. That's partly due to the fact that writing for television, film or novels is all about quality and mastering the craft. It takes time, dedication and a whole lot of patience and humility. You're going to need great characters to create a strong emotional connection with your audience.

When I was four, my dad read Tolkien to me every night. It's difficult to remember much about that time in my life. Aside from the theft of my bouncy toy from our apartment in Cholet, France, I mostly recall the stories. More specifically, I remember memorable character moments. One of the earliest of these is Tolkien's Black Rider chasing Frodo and Sam as they leave the Shire. I remember exactly where I was—propped up in bed, tucked in beside my brother with my constant companion, a blanket named Picker. Jonathan held on to his teddy bear, Ben, who by now had an overextended neck due to being clutched around the throat on a regular basis. The right side of the bed touched up against the wall and our father sat to our left.

I recall listening to the moment when Frodo and Sam hide beneath an outcrop at the side of the road. The Rider dismounts, breathes hoarsely...and sniffs. Bugs swarm all over the ground. I imagined Frodo and Sam's hearts pounding in fear. And the Rider sniffs, trying to catch their scent. (I held my breath until the Ring Wraith got back on his horse and rode off.)

As my dad read to me, I was intrigued just as much by what Tolkien put into words as he left to my imagination. I had experienced what Roland Barthes refers to as a "writerly text" (*texte scriptible*)—one that invites the reader to participate, at least to some degree through an active act of imagination, in the writing of the story. In contrast, the "readerly text" (or *texte lisible*) washes over us, to be consumed as is. By inviting me to co-create with him, Tolkien had caught me up in the emotional core of the story. I understood that the quest to destroy the ring was dangerous; the very lives of Frodo and Sam were at risk. Without the Rider, without his cloak and hollowness, without his quirky, distinctive sniff, I may not have carried that experience with me for over thirty years. The ominous Black Rider precipitated my emotional connection to the story and made the protagonist's jeopardy overwhelmingly real.

That, in a nutshell, is why character matters. Empower the reader's imagination and your characters will take on a life of their own. That said, I'd like to offer a few words of caution. Bringing a character to life is a balancing act. On one hand, you'll have to do a lot of invisible background work. Who is your protagonist? What does she do for a living? How is her family life? How did she grow up? How does she relate to other people? We've already considered these kinds of questions in previous chapters. That's what we call *backstory*.

Before actually writing your script, you'll need a keen sense of how your principle character and also the antagonist got to where they are when the story begins. As we say in Ireland, they didn't just float up the Liffey in a bubble. Thus, they shouldn't act as though they did. Prior to showing up in your story, all of the characters had lives, experiences, fears and motivations that made them who they are now. Something got them to this point…at this time…in this place. This brings us to the *why*.

More important than the physical description of your character and of her world is the *why:* Why is she the way she is? Why did she get to this place? Why does she relate as she does to others? Learn to think in terms of *why* rather than *what* and you'll learn to reveal the nuances of your character through action instead of wordy dialogue and exposition. A great character never reveals too much about herself through dialogue. Nor should she encounter the people she sees on a regular basis as though she's meeting them for the first time. As a writer, you have to balance what you know about the character with what you ought to reveal. Introducing a great character is like dating. You have to retain enough mystery to engage the audience.

If you're doing your job right and spending lots of time with the character, you'll eventually face the reality that she's going to grow up, get a mind of her own, and start doing things you never for a moment anticipated. Just go with it. Once your character breathes and lives of her own accord, your job, as William Faulkner put it, is to run around behind her and write down what she does.

Creating great characters isn't about control. It's about groundwork, research, and allowing them room to breathe. If you do a good job in developing the characters in your movie, novel or stage play, there will come a point that they'll surprise you.

♦ Exercise 21. *By now you should have a good idea of the values at stake in your story.*

1. What are the underdog values? What are the dominant values?
2. When all is said and done, what is at stake on the internal, external and philosophical levels?

♦ Exercise 22. *Let's think more about your protagonist.*

1. Who is she (or he)? Does she have some kind of defining quirk?
2. What is most dear to her? Why is this important?
3. What defining moment in her past helps to explain how she got where she is now?
4. Jot down all the elements that make up the protagonist's daily routine. What are the two or three most important aspects of day-to-day life that will help the audience understand the protagonist's ordinary world?
5. What is your character's want? What is it that she doesn't know about herself yet that holds her back? What is her need? With respect to the stakes of the story, why is this

important? How must the protagonist overcome her want to understand and respond to her need?

♦ Exercise 23. *Let's talk antagonist.*

1. Something in your antagonist's past set him on the course to where he finds himself when we turn the cameras on. What is it? Why is this significant?
2. What does your antagonist want? How does that conflict with what your protagonist wants?
3. If your antagonist is to be redeemed, rather than defeated, what is his need? How might he go about learning that need?

♦ Exercise 24. *I want you to imagine your protagonist and antagonist are journaling the night before your story begins.*

1. What do they write about? (Alternatively, you might envision a letter to a loved one.) In one page or less, articulate, in the first person, the worldview of each character.
2. What does each believe? How did they come to believe this? Keep in mind that your antagonist is not (in most cases) a madman. He has a very real and very grounded rationale that undergirds everything he does. For your audience to connect emotionally with the antagonist, you also must connect.

♦ Exercise 25. *Let's think about the character arc.*

1. When the opportunity for change presents itself, why does the protagonist resist that change?
2. What will it take to induce the dilemma? In other words,

how might you escalate conflict in order to put the protagonist between a rock and a hard place?

3. What single event will cause the protagonist to commit to the quest and cross the threshold into Act Two? Make sure your character doesn't just get swept along in the currents of the story. Remember, the protagonist must make a firm commitment to moving forward. Is this reflected in your story building blocks?

STEP 13. MORE CHARACTER BASICS

Think about your favorite movie characters. What makes them so endearing to you?

Do you remember what they were doing when you met them? What did they want? Did they achieve that end, or did they realize they needed something else over the course of the movie? Is what drew you in at the beginning the same as what made you love them at the end? (I'll venture the answer is "No.")

In AS GOOD AS IT GETS, we meet Melvin consumed with his business as usual—writing romance novels. Very quickly, we realize he has less empathy than a robot and utter contempt for anything to do with love. When his neighbor's fluffy white dog ventures into the corridor and disturbs Melvin, he coaxes it to approach, grabs it…and shoves it down a garbage chute. Here is a man riddled with inner conflict. He mocks the public's taste for romance, yet writes about it with gusto. Even so, Melvin feels the need (unbeknownst to him) to connect with others—even if that means driving them crazy with his peculiarities.

All great characters suffer from an inner conflict to which they are, in the beginning, oblivious. What makes Melvin's love interest, Carol, special is that she can see through his harsh exterior and gets to know the man behind the mask. As he opens up to her ever so begrudgingly, Melvin recognizes the loneliness and longing to be with another person. He could never have imagined having such feelings at the beginning of the story. It takes Melvin losing Carol to come to this realization and recognize his need. In so doing, he finds the strength to wrestle against his original worldview in order to win her back. In the end, Melvin's need for love is stronger than his want for independence. And there you have it: Character arc conveys a journey from want to need.

Let's go back to Aristotle for a moment. I want to focus on a concept he develops in the *Nicomachean Ethics*. If you've ever read a synopsis of *Ethics*, you've encountered the idea that virtues, according to Aristotle, are habits. This leads to the common misinterpretation that virtue must be practiced over and over until it becomes simple routine. But for Aristotle, moral virtue is an active condition that entails a pro-active decision every single time—virtue, therefore, manifests itself in action. An action can be virtuous only when a person holds himself in what Aristotle terms a stable equilibrium of the soul (rather than under the duress of passion or other emotions). For Aristotle, that equilibrium is what constitutes a person's character in the broader, philosophical sense of the word.

In the beginning of insanely great stories, the protagonist lives in a state of artificial or feigned equilibrium. Whether he knows it and feels restless (like Luke Skywalker) or thinks everyone else is the problem (like Melvin), every key moment of the story will challenge the protagonist to reach a true equilibrium. Sometimes, your character is going to make progress. At others, she will come close to unraveling. Upon hitting the brick wall, it might even seem that she reaches a point of no return. By pushing through that brick wall and achieving the moment of self-realization, the protagonist achieves meaningful equilibrium and crosses over into Act Three—ready, at last, to defeat the antagonist or find true love. (Hence why, for me, the brick wall and transition to the final act are experienced as one single moment in the story design, rather than as a series of events.)

Rage, jealousy, envy, revenge: These are all sentiments that throw the protagonist off-kilter. For example, GLADIATOR's Maximus is thrown off course by revenge. He must overcome that thirst to become, instead, the champion of the Rome Marcus Aurelius envisioned—a free Rome, given back to the people. In BRAVEHEART, too, William Wallace achieves his ultimate equilibrium by laying down his life for the future of Scotland. To accomplish his goal and maintain that new equilibrium demands that he has his wits about him; he can't drink the princess's potion as it would numb his senses and mind. At his end, Wallace—like Maximus—is freed from the thirst for revenge. Hence, he can die with "freedom" on his lips, inspiring Robert the Bruce to carry on the fight in the name of that which is bigger than both of them: "You bled with Wallace, now bleed with me." (I love that line. Thank you, Randall Wallace.)

And who can forget Rick in CASABLANCA? Rick is the archetypal yet completely unique man embittered by lost love. He doesn't stick his neck out for anyone. But when Ilsa walks into his bar, his fabricated equilibrium shatters. Rick drinks. He insults Ilsa. He rejects her. However, Rick moves beyond self-pity, gets back in the fight and achieves such a state of equilibrium that he can "do the thinking for both" of them. In the final scene, Rick puts Ilsa on the plane because he thinks clearly for the first time in a very long time. Healed of past hurts, he embraces his newly achieved, unflappable equilibrium and becomes a hero in his own right.

As we have seen, the achievement of equilibrium (as Aristotle described it in the *Nicomachean Ethics*) is key to understanding the great character arc. When we encounter the protagonist in Act One, she has likely achieved a façade of stability and equilibrium just to get by. The inciting incident then knocks a few holes in that façade and the dilemma demolishes it. The search for a new equilibrium has begun. In Act Two, the protagonist alternates between embracing and refusing a new façade. Most likely, she embraces it for all the wrong reasons. For example, Maximus doesn't fully commit to fighting in the arena until he learns it may enable him to stand in front of Commodus and exact his revenge. To enter Act Three, the protagonist commits to a new equilibrium. This commitment is tested one last time during the final confrontation with the antagonist—and in most cases, it's unwavering. Begin with a want, end with a need: Achieving the new equilibrium is what meaningful character arc is all about. Michael Hauge has great things to say about the relationship of character arc to Jungian psychology in *Writing Screenplays That Sell*. I recommend you check out his thoughts on this subject, too. And read what my good friends John Bucher and Jeremy Casper have to say about how the inside journey complements the outside one in *The Inside Out Story*.

- Exercise 26. *Brainstorm three or four attempts the antagonist will make to thwart the protagonist's progress towards the MacGuffin. Think of these in terms of a chain of action and reaction. The protagonist does A, which in turn causes the antagonist to do B, which causes the protagonist to do C… and so on.*

- Exercise 27. *When the protagonist hits the brick wall and is on the verge of giving up…*

    1. What inner transformation must she face to continue the quest?
    2. Why could she not see this sooner? Why does she face the moment of self-realization now?

- Exercise 28. *When the protagonist faces off against the antagonist in Act Three…*

    1. What has changed?
    2. How will the antagonist dig deep to quash this final uprising?
    3. In the last critical moment, when it seems that the protagonist will never win, how will we recognize on-screen that the power dynamic has shifted?
    4. How will the protagonist win out?

- Exercise 29. *At the end of the adventure, taking into account the stakes you articulated in Exercise 21…*

    1. What is the single most significant thing to have changed in the story world?

2. Brainstorm two or three effective ways to make this change clear (i.e., visually communicated) on-screen.

Before moving on to the specifics of character introductions, I'd like to share a few thoughts about backstory. It's in the past for a reason. As I mentioned above, your protagonist doesn't appear for the first time halfway down page one. She has an independent existence in the world of the story and it's your job to know and understand it.

Let's step out of our discussion of character for a moment to glean a tip from the world of production design and animation. A few years ago, I had the good fortune of chatting with Doug Rogers, who designed the world of SHREK, for which he won an academy award, and TANGLED (2010). Doug explained to me that production design, especially in animation, is an exciting yet daunting task. In the age of the computer, all that exists are the animated frames of the movie. (And as CGI becomes more and more the norm for live action, we can expect the same to apply to other films, too.) Doug's job and passion is to create a world so believable, so holistic, so captivating that someone looking at the screen sees a hill (or part of it) in the frame and automatically envisions it extending outside of that frame. A good production designer therefore creates the illusion that, if we shifted the camera slightly left, it would reveal more of the landscape or setting, when in fact there's nothing there—nothing at all. In other words, great production designers like Doug offer us a slice of the story world that conjures in our imagination a vast and expansive universe.

Think about it. You don't see much of Tatooine in the original STAR WARS. Yet, from what you do see, you conjure up a broader idea of Luke's home planet. And most of the scenes in CASABLANCA (adapted, we might add, from a stage-play) unfold at Rick's café, with an occasional excursion to the market or streets. And yet, you can probably tell me a lot about that world, too. FROZEN (2013) presents only a few snapshots of Arundel, but viewers can describe Anna and Elsa's world in detail.

My point is that developing a great character for the screen, or, for that matter, in a novel, is much like the work of a skilled production designer. Present a well-chosen slice of the character's life, then leave the rest up to the audience's imagination.

Where does this leave us in terms of backstory? The simple answer is that you shouldn't reveal too much of it, nor should you do so all at once. Instead, backstory helps you gauge how your characters are likely to respond to the events that arise over the course of the plot. Backstory offers us another way character and plot are intertwined. Everything that happens over the course of the story—each event, interaction, conversation—provides an opportunity to reveal the inner character as your protagonist reacts and responds. Oftentimes, some backstory is necessary for a setup that will be paid off later in the story. Or perhaps you want to present some key information about the protagonist's past that explains the decision she'll make at the midpoint. There are many ways to get this information across in the script. For example, you might stage a conversation in which your protagonist is pressed by another character to reveal critical information. (Making your protagonist reluctant to comply is key to making this transfer of information seem more natural on-screen. It also adds to the conflict of your scene.) Find ways to present information in exciting, integrated ways.

Remember how RAIDERS OF THE LOST ARK (1981) achieves this? Near the beginning, Indiana Jones pulls out an old book to explain the story of the Ark of the Covenant. The setting of the large lecture hall provides a grand esthetic and illustrations in the book ensure the Ark's history is shown on screen—and not only discussed by the characters. *Show, don't tell.*

When it comes to learning how to pull off the integration of backstory and exposition, new animated classics have it covered. Take, for example, the exposition sequence at the beginning of UP (2009). The writers cover decades of backstory in less than seven minutes of screen time. The whole sequence is heartfelt—tear-jerking, even—and we know everything we need to know about Carl by the time Russell shows up on his doorstep. In a similar vein, FINDING NEMO soars with an emotional pre-credits sequence. In

Basics of Story Design

just over three minutes, we bear witness as Marlin loses his wife and 399 of his unborn children. If that doesn't solicit compassion and emotion, you might require some sensitivity training. And what about FROZEN's delightful snowman song (dubbed the "exposition song" in the Honest Frozen spoof trailer)? It carries us through Anna and Elsa's childhood and drops us right where we need to be in time for coronation day. Notice how they remind us that today is that special day. Anna wakes up in a less than graceful state, sees her dress and squeals with delight. That the coronation is about to begin is reinforced yet again when the little boy in the square expresses his distaste for dressing up—and once more when Anna hears the bells after her meet-cute with Hans. As Richard Walter rightly notes in *Essentials of Screenwriting*, integration is key. Nothing happens by accident in a great screenplay. Every detail is programmed to drive the story forward. If backstory is important to something that happens later, find an unexpected and meaningful way to present it. Otherwise, leave it in the past.

STEP 14. MAKING A SPLASH

You get one chance to introduce your protagonist. Make it count.

We don't need to know about the color of her hair, how tall she is, what she's wearing, or for that matter, that she has a scar above her left eye—unless this information is integrated (i.e., decisive for shaping the story). We should also note that using dialogue to introduce your character's backstory is equally ineffective, awkward and unbelievable. What we want is to feel like we're catching the protagonist right in the midst of day-to-day life. That's what the old playwrights meant when they strove to begin *in media res* ("in the middle of things").

The very first scene is your golden chance to introduce the protagonist through action. Show, don't tell, who she is. What are her endearing traits? What drives her? These are a few questions to ask before your character steps onto the page. The audience also joins the action *in media res*. They must believe the movie begins because someone turned the cameras on—the filmmakers pick a moment to begin, but the story is already well underway. The human being we encounter on-screen is a complex one, about to be called on a new journey.

In BBC's SHERLOCK (2010), Dr. Watson and Sherlock Holmes have separate lives underway and a rich history before they collide. It's precisely the sum of their experiences confronting each other when they first meet that creates the potential for something great to happen—a story big bang, of sorts. Two entirely different people come together and journey forward together on a series of unlikely and exciting adventures. Over the course of that journey, Sherlock changes John and John changes Sherlock.

Let's take a closer look at one of my favorite character introductions. In RAIDERS OF THE LOST ARK, the cameras turn on in the midst of an exotic jungle near the foot of a jagged peak. The as-of-yet unknown Indiana Jones steps into view first, wearing his weathered, trademark hat. (The hat is integrated: It's part of what makes him distinct. He dons it on every adventure.) Note how the director gives the secondary characters their cameo introductions, too. By doing so, we sense they'll be important. Suspense builds. The secondary characters provide a contrast to Indy. Whereas the hero is calm, collected and put together, the others are sweaty and take great pains to keep up with him. The man out front with the hat is different.

The trek through the jungle continues. The local guide cuts back vegetation and reveals a carving in the rock. He runs away; Indy, meanwhile, approaches, fearless. The marker has something to do with what he is seeking. Again, suspense builds. Indy pauses. He picks up a dart and casts it aside. Indy is not a man who backs down in the face of adversity. A secondary character takes a closer look and tastes the tip: "The poison is fresh." Jeopardy builds—this is a dangerous mission and enemies lurk nearby. We arrive by a large pool in the river. One of the secondary characters betrays Jones and pulls out a revolver. However, Indy is quick to draw his whip and rid his adversary of the weapon. The traitor scampers away. Once again, all of these actions reveal Indy's character.

With only one helper left, Indy continues to the entrance of the temple. The jeopardy rises further when we hear Indy speak for the first time. He reveals that this is as far as his competitor made it. No one has come out of this temple alive. But Indy is no novice. He fills a bag with sand—presumably because he anticipates a thing or two about the obstacles he might encounter inside the cave. (He is a high-powered researcher and specialist, after all.) Note that Indy doesn't explain any of his actions. The writer, Laurence Kasdan, leaves it up to the viewers to draw their own conclusions. The result? We want to know more. We're engrossed. He's got our attention.

Basics of Story Design

Next, we find ourselves in a spooky, dark tunnel with Indy and the one secondary character following behind. Indy remains calm and determined; the other man's fear is palpable. Indy encounters an obstacle—tarantulas on his back. He couldn't care less. He brushes them off with his whip. We wonder, is there anything of which this man is afraid? (As it turns out, we find out he hates snakes and this is all the more amusing because of the contrast provided by the spiders.) A bright patch of light enters the chambers ahead. Indy recognizes a trap and instructs his companion to "stay out of the light." He goes to investigate. Sure enough, it's a trap. When Indy ventures a hand to cut off the beam, deadly spikes spring out from both walls. Impaled upon the spikes is the skeleton of Indy's competitor. Still, Indy remains calm. (His helper, meanwhile, screams in terror.)

On to the next obstacle: The passageway gives way to a bottomless pit. Undaunted, Indiana Jones uses his whip to spring across. His companion clearly has less experience in such matters and all but falls in. Once again, this builds Indy up. It serves another purpose, too. When the companion almost falls in, Indy saves him—a fitting setup for the betrayal that will occur shortly after. We reach the final obstacle: the threat of a deadly arrow that Indy clears adeptly. At last, we are in the presence of the object Indy seeks—the golden icon. Having estimated the icon's weight, Indy pulls some sand from his sack and swaps the sack out for the icon. Genius! He seems to be out of the woods, but we realize soon enough that Indy miscalculated the statue's weight. The whole place crumbles around him. Dodging arrows and jumping right over another pit, Indy runs for his life. As the temple door closes, his companion betrays him and forces Indy to give up the icon. Indy escapes in the nick of time, leaps over the giant pit (without the aid of his whip this time) and rolls under the door. On the other side, he finds the man who betrayed him dead, done in by one of the traps. He regains the idol momentarily but will be forced to give it up, again, when he exits the pyramid—this time to his arch nemesis, Belloq. There's little chance now that we will forget Belloq's face. The antagonist has made his entry.

The entire opening sequence of **RAIDERS OF THE LOST ARK**

reveals the protagonist's character through action. We also know what the movie is about. This will be a tale of adventure, courage and betrayal. We, like Indy, must learn to trust no one. If you haven't seen RAIDERS, tonight is a good time to watch.

◆   Exercise 30. *Revisit the opening scene of your movie.*

1. Brainstorm two or three alternatives to increase the curb appeal of your opening scene. How can you make it more exciting, quirky, adventurous or endearing—all the while revealing the protagonist's character through action? Great writers rarely settle for their initial idea. And when they do, they work to elevate that idea and make it pop.
2. You've seen in RAIDERS OF THE LOST ARK an important aspect of scene mechanics at work, taught by Hal Ackerman in *Write Screenplays That Sell*. Before the protagonist reaches a goal inside a scene (e.g., to get the idol), she must encounter approximately three obstacles of heightened difficulty. Brainstorm ways to introduce such obstacles into your opening scene. (This is an important principle, and I recommend you learn to apply it throughout your story.)
3. What defining trait or trademark possession might you give your protagonist, similar to Indy's hat?

STEP 15. COMPARE AND CONTRAST

Building great characters requires the integration of contrasts and contradictions.

    We're going to stay with RAIDERS OF THE LOST ARK today, as the scenes that unfold next display a remarkable contrast to those we discussed yesterday. At the same time, these scenes continue to reveal more about the complexity of Indiana Jones as a leading character. The writing is masterful—and quite fun, to boot.
    After the opening sequence, RAIDERS gives us a second establishing shot. It marks a vivid contrast to the world of the jungle—manicured lawns and collegiate gothic. Presumably we find ourselves at a distinguished school in the Northeast. We reconnect with Indy in front of a blackboard, wearing professional garb, complete with bow tie, glasses, and tweed jacket. He's teaching anthropology. Ah, we think. So this is his day job. Note how all of the information above is communicated without a single line of dialogue. The classroom is also filled with almost exclusively attractive young women. One of them has "Love you" written in eyeliner across her eyelids. As she blinks to reveal her message, Indy is visibly uncomfortable. We sense he doesn't really have a way with women, although he doubtless has what it takes to be a womanizer. He comes across as a man of integrity, uncomfortable with the young woman's flirtation—a nice setup that will soon contrast with his ex-lover slapping him in a bar. As it turns out, Indiana is indeed clueless about women.
    Like a typical professor, Dr. Jones assigns homework at the end of

class and students bustle out. If we hadn't witnessed the opening adventure, the protagonist would come across as a mild-mannered college professor with highly specialized textbook knowledge of anthropology. His is, in appearance, a normal life. Since we are privy to other information, we find Indy exciting and intriguing. Is adventuring in the jungle what professors get up to when school's out for summer?

Great characters are often persons of many contradictions. Keep in mind that those apparent contradictions are simply different facets of a complex personality. Reconciling the fragments and applying them towards the greater good—linked to the character's sense of calling—are one of the key functions of the adventure, or, for that matter, love story (if it's a romance). The transformation from fragmented to integrated persona constitutes the character arc.

In the next scene of RAIDERS, Kasdan introduces the specific goal—the MacGuffin—of the story: Find the Ark of the Covenant before the Nazis do. The scene unfolds in an impressive lecture hall. Two U.S. government officials have come to consult with Dr. Jones and his friend, the dean. The first thing I want you to take away from this scene is that we're not merely forgiving of the exposition that takes place. In fact, we're very open to it. By now, we desire it. This is because the writer has done his job well. By getting us emotionally invested in the high-thrill ride of the opening adventure sequence and presenting us with the contrasting world of the university, we want to know more, and not only about the story—about the character. Character likeability is key, but it's not enough. Whether good or bad, friend or foe, you need the reader and audience invested emotionally in your protagonist. In other words, the lecture hall scene (where we are first introduced to the Ark of the Covenant) works not because it's a cool setting (although that certainly doesn't hurt), nor because the characters on screen read from an old book and show us the drawings (which nonetheless contributes to the authority of Dr. Jones). The scene works because it provides us with a glimpse into how Indiana navigates the gulf between his two lives—Harvard professor by day, renegade tomb raider by night.

Moreover, the scene contributes to the development of Indy's character. His influence goes so far as to command the respect of the U.S. government. When the Nazis are digging in the Middle East, the government consults with Dr. Jones. He's their go-to guy. While he no doubt enjoys to some degree his reputation as a subject matter expert, we further get the sense that Indy isn't in the adventure just for himself. He serves something greater than a personal agenda, greater than his research, greater than the needs of individual governments. Indy is the kind of man who fights for causes larger than himself. He believes in science and in truth—he's a true hero who stirs within us the desire to be something greater than we are. Thus, the character's call to action becomes our call to action. Before we know it, we're along for the ride. The emotional tie established up front between the protagonist and the audience carries us through the whole movie.

Keep in mind that Indy's quest is also very personal. Kasdan carefully reminds us that Belloq (the arch-nemesis who took the golden idol from Indy during the opening sequence) is assisting the Nazis. Now, Indy can have his revenge. Thus, by the inciting incident, RAIDERS OF THE LOST ARK has clearly established three levels of stakes for the story:

(1) *The personal stakes*: Will Dr. Jones beat Belloq and have his revenge? Is he up to the task? Although we like Indy, we saw Belloq outwit him in the opening sequence. Indy's starting out as the underdog.

(2) *The external stakes*: Can Jones prevent the Nazis from retrieving the Ark and bringing the whole world to its knees? Note that most of us (I hope) know how World War II plays out, so the real question isn't whether or not the Nazis will be stopped—it's how the story unfolds that interests us.

(3) *The philosophical stakes*: Will goodness and courage triumph over self-interest and evil? Can the underdog values win out amidst the cynical world of war?

We haven't unpacked all of the ways in which RAIDERS OF THE LOST ARK wins big in introducing character. There's a lot to say about supporting characters, too. But you should be beginning to get the idea. And now, you just need to think about how to apply these techniques to your own story.

- Exercise 31. *Confronting the blank page.* It's important to keep in mind that you're a seasoned consumer of movies. That means you're typically watching a movie and then drawing conclusions from what you see on-screen. When you confront the blank page, you have to work through the design process in reverse—think of what you want the audience to deduce and craft the moment from which they will make their deductions.

    1. Go back to the script you were reading throughout the earlier steps. How did the screenwriter craft moments and events that would allow the audience to make deductions about the protagonist's character? Define at least three of these moments.
    2. Now, think of the protagonist in your movie. What are some of the characteristics that make up his or her personality? Brainstorm two or three ways to render that part of their personality on screen.
    3. You know your character better than all of us. In your movie, what's the protagonist's pressure point? How might you activate that pressure point over the course of the story? Brainstorm three or four ways to escalate pressure so that it might be difficult for your character to make clear decisions.

- Exercise 32. *Be sure to revisit your beats for tomorrow. Make any necessary adjustments, and if you have time, relax by watching a movie and mulling over everything you've learned!*

STEP 16. TO OUTLINE!

All good things come to those who wait.

If you're chomping at the bit to get started, don't fret. When it comes to screenwriting, the vast majority of the work gets done before you write your first scene. For some, it's a question of jumping straight in, getting the ideas out and outlining later. Whatever your approach may be, you're going to have to outline at some point—and probably more than once—if you want your screenplay to be the best it can be. Personally, I prefer to invest my time in outlining up front. Even after completing your first draft, knowing how to take your story back down to outline can make the revision process all the more productive. By working on the backbone of the story, rather than massaging the surface, you'll be able to identify key issues quickly and empower yourself to find solutions to them.

Think of your *step outline* as a complete, scene-by-scene outline of your movie. Some people like to work on this using index cards. If you elect to follow that method, you should dedicate one card per scene, and then lay them out and switch them around until you're happy with the general look and feel of your story. However, that method made much more sense in the age of the typewriter than it does now. Computer software makes the step outline process much easier. The bottom line? Find a method that works for you. In this chapter, I outline what works for me. You can adapt to suit. Whatever approach you take, the goal will remain the same: to end up with an industry-standard step outline that takes you from "fade in" to "fade out."

My preference is to outline using my usual screenwriting software. If you're a student or educator, there are some great discounts available to you for commercial products. There are also some free, or inexpensive formatting tools you can download online.

Before you jump into outlining, let's cover some basic formatting. For each scene you write, you'll need to create a *slug line*. Here, you indicate whether the scene takes place inside (INT) or outside (EXT), the specific location and whether it takes place during the DAY or NIGHT. You needn't be more specific than that, nor should you clutter up the page by indicating that it's "CONTINUOUS," meaning simply that the scene in question occurs immediately after the preceding scene. Your reader will assume that to be the case unless you change from DAY to NIGHT. Some of you will have noticed already that I omit periods after INT and EXT. That's not in error. During my classes at UCLA, I adopted the formatting preferences of Richard Walter. (Final Draft includes a "Richard Walter" template or you can simply override manually the addition of periods.) I like Richard's approach that aims for minimalism—nothing to distract us from the words on the page that merit our attention. When it comes to having your screenplay read by the studios, this kind of esthetic counts. It means business. At the end of the day, you are of course free to adopt whatever formatting choices you like. With all of this in mind, a slug line for one of my scripts might look like this:

> INT   GROCERY STORE   DAY
> (or)
> EXT   FOREST   NIGHT

Now, let's focus on formatting specifics inside the scene itself. Don't get lost in lengthy passages of description. You really want to define who your character is by what we see them doing, not by how you describe their environment to us. For example, I could describe at great length a coffee shop in Austin and the people in it, from what they're wearing to the way their hair is cut. But that serves little purpose. Instead, I want to look for a way to distill everything about that place into a pithy statement that grabs the attention of the reader and allows us to focus, instead, on what the protagonist (or other key character introduced) is up to:

INT   COFFEE SHOP   DAY

Writers and coders congregate at tables.
Hipster heaven. Behind the counter, JOE (35) mans the espresso machine. On the counter, his phone BUZZES with an incoming text.
A CUSTOMER (28) checks her watch.

    CUSTOMER
Could I get that to go this morning, maybe.

    JOE
Hmmm.

    CUSTOMER
My mocha. I'm going to miss the train.

    JOE
I'll be right with you.

The machine HISSES and emits steam. Joe jumps to attention. It explodes coffee all over him.

In the sample from a scene above, you'll notice that I keep description to a minimum. I also pick a gender-specific name: Joe. That saves me the need of explaining he's a man. All we need now is to include Joe's age, in parentheses right after his name. Joe's attention is divided between the coffee he serves up and the message that comes in on his phone. (I capitalize the BUZZ of the phone to indicate that we hear the noise on-screen.) To add pressure to the situation, we give Joe an impatient customer who's about to miss her train. Still, he ignores her. To make matters worse, the espresso machine explodes all over the place. We've yet to find out what the message received by Joe entails—and perhaps we'll withhold it from the reader or viewer for a while, adding to the suspense. For now, we know the contents of the message must be important enough for Joe to become distracted, ignore his customer, and fail to notice the malfunction of the espresso machine. We don't say any of that; *we show it*. In step outline format, the above scene might be rendered:

> INT   COFFEE SHOP   DAY
>
>> Writers and coders congregate at tables.
>> Hipster heaven. Behind the counter, JOE (35)
>> mans the espresso machine. On the counter,
>> his phone BUZZES with an incoming text.
>> A CUSTOMER (28) checks her watch. Joe
>> is so distracted by the message that he doesn't
>> notice the espresso machine HISS. It explodes
>> all over him.

If an important line of dialogue jumps out at me, I include that in my outline by placing it between quotes and underlining it for future reference.

Before going any further, let's run a quick test to determine whether or not the scenes you have outlined will actually function as scenes. (We will have time to elevate them even further later. For now, we just care about them being acceptable.)

In its most rudimentary form, a scene consists of a setup (what's going on when the scene begins), an event (something that happens in the scene) and a result. That result is typically expressed in terms of how the protagonist reacts to the event and how the other characters in the scene react to the protagonist. It could also encompass how the secondary characters react and how the protagonist reacts to them. In other words, just like movies, individual scenes must have a beginning, middle and end. Moreover, throughout this process, the scene must accomplish one of two things —or in a best case scenario, both. On one hand, it should contribute to the character development. On the other, it should move the plot forward (whether this in fact carries the protagonist closer to or further away from her goal).

Finally, I'll point out an issue most inexperienced screenwriters face when they write scenes, brought to my attention by Hal Ackerman. (If you can't take his UCLA class, you should read his book, *Write Screenplays That Sell*.) Your protagonist enters every scene with a want, or desire. Too often, in early versions of scripts, the character fulfills that want without sufficient opposition.

Let's use my coffee-shop example above. Perhaps my character, Joe, has just found out that his girlfriend, Helena, is leaving him for good. She has even gone so far as to tell him that there's no point talking to her. Joe suspects this is the fault of Helena's brother, Charles, who doesn't like Joe much. (What he doesn't realize, however, is that Helena is a secret agent who has just been activated for an important mission and she's trying to let him down easy. Over the course of our story, he's going to find that out by stumbling into the middle of the mission and getting himself kidnapped by the bad guys.) Instead of sticking around to clean up the coffee machine, Joe immediately dials Charles, whose secretary picks up. She recognizes Joe's number from the caller ID, informs Joe never to call again and hangs up on him. But Joe will not be so easily defeated. To the shock of his impatient customer, Joe vaults over the top of the counter and runs out the door. In his own way, Joe just overcame and responded to obstacle #1—"He doesn't want to talk to you, and never call here again."

But when Joe gets out in the streets of Austin, it's rush hour. There are cars everywhere. Undeterred, Joe dodges between moving vehicles and almost gets run over. (He just overcame obstacle #2.) He runs into the office block and up to Charles's office, where Charles's administrative assistant attempts to stop him, to no avail. (That's obstacle #3.) He runs down the corridor to find an empty office. Where did Charles go? A door in the bookshelves, cracked open, reveals a secret passageway.

Joe never achieves his goal of speaking to Charles in the scene described above. However, he has found out that there's more to

Charles than meets the eye—after all, what kind of person has secret passageways leading out of their office and why did Charles run? What I've illustrated here is a well-known writing technique that Hal Ackerman refers to as the red light/green light principle. In order to build suspense in a scene, it's helpful to throw three clear obstacles at the protagonist. This is especially significant for the major plot beats. You want them to pop and keep the audience on the edge of their seats.

- ◆ Exercise 33. *This is a good time to revisit the scenes you created for the major story beats when you developed your story worksheet. I encourage you today to take up the scenes you came up with and revise them until you're happy with the basic structure of each plot beat. This will become the foundation of your complete step outline.*

STEP 17. PLEASE MIND THE GAP

You've made it this far. Now for the final push.

All that's left for you to do is to fill in the gaps in your step outline. As you've no doubt realized, the hard work you've invested over the first fifteen steps to writing an insanely great screenplay is paying off!

Don't be daunted by the task ahead. Now is the time to settle down and visualize the end of your story design process: a clearly outlined screenplay, from beginning to end. By the time you start writing scenes, you'll have a bird's eye view of everything you hope to accomplish. It can be intimidating to think of outlining sixty or so scenes, all in a row. Thankfully, you don't have to do that. All you have to do is think in terms of your tent-pole moments. By now you've settled on an opening image (two to three minutes or pages). You have a clear outline of how the inciting incident will unfold (two to three minutes or pages). To fill out the set-up sequence, you only have to create three or four more scenes (seven to nine minutes or pages) to fill in the gap.

Over that setup sequence, you need to accomplish certain goals. First of all, make sure the protagonist and antagonist get great, personal, unique introductions. Second, communicate the key elements of the protagonist's world. What does she want? What does she need? How is she blind to that need and how does her blindness affect others without her realizing it? (You can look over your homework from earlier chapters in order to complete this process.) The key is to not settle. Don't go for the first idea that pops into your head. If you're writing a romantic comedy, dream up a new and unique setting for the meet-cute. Give us characters that, while familiar, are entirely new to us and quirky. If science fiction is your passion, set up the world and how it is different from ours. And especially, whatever you do, don't forget that your reader and audience must sense that a storm is brewing. Something is just off-kilter—although the protagonist probably doesn't know it yet. Keep in mind that you are going to have to make choices. You have a limited number of pages to get all this information across in the most interesting, "show-don't-tell" fashion possible.

- Exercise 34. *Go for it! Map out the scenes between the opening image and the inciting incident. Be sure to identify, as you did previously, the setup, event and outcome of each scene. Where does the conflict lie? How does the conflict build from scene to scene? Make sure that every scene pushes the story towards the inciting incident. It all comes down to that one moment.*

Your next goal is to fill in the gap from the inciting incident to the dilemma and right on up to the end of Act One. You'll probably have just one or two scenes that slide in between the inciting incident and the dilemma (three at most). Then you'll need around three or four scenes to carry you up to the first act break (i.e., the end of the first act).

- Exercise 35. *Using the inciting incident and the dilemma, and then the dilemma and the end of Act One as your tent-pole moments, fill in the gaps to complete Act One. Be sure to test all of the scenes you construct and elevate them as much as possible. Why does the protagonist resist the call to adventure (or romance)? What happens to change her mind? How can you set up that change? In what ways can you gently raise the stakes in the final section of Act One so as to carry the protagonist into the first act break and force a decision?*

Great! We're now in the first half of the second act, in the thick of the adventure sequence (between crossing the threshold and the midpoint), when things will start to turn downhill for the protagonist. It's time to have some fun. A lot of movies lose momentum in this sequence. The key is to rely on your supporting character to introduce new levels of tension into the narrative. Blake Snyder, in *Save the Cat*, calls this section the "fun and games." That's because your protagonist will likely experience a series of successes and progress towards their goal. It's typically a segment of the movie that's fun and entertaining for the audience. Meeting the supporting character helps to point the protagonist in the right direction. As Blake notes, this is also the point of the story at which "set pieces" were typically introduced into screenplays.

Back in the day, when movies were shot primarily on studio lots and CGI was but the figment of someone's imagination, movie sets were constructed in the studios. Given the cost of such projects, police stations, restaurants, office space and the like could be recycled. From time to time, though, a scene in a movie was deemed exciting enough to warrant the construction of a set. That scene became known as a "set piece." We still use the term today—both in theory and in practice. For example, when Brad Bird was filming MISSION IMPOSSIBLE: GHOST PROTOCOL (2011), the Dubai climbing stunt (originally scheduled to be shot using CGI) was deemed so exciting that it merited the cost of being shot on location. That's a set piece. More and more, we find them in the opening of movies, too, for example the plane attack at the beginning of THE DARK KNIGHT RISES (2012).

Whatever your topic and genre, the first half of Act Two needs to be exciting and keep the audience invested. At the same time, you need to make sure the protagonist is progressing towards her goal. I find it helpful to think of three sequences, or series of scenes, that make up mini-adventures to help get me from the act break to the midpoint. It's helpful, too, if the mini-adventures build one upon the other in intensity. I also want to make sure that the antagonist is making plans to reverse the protagonist's successes. As in the beginning of Act One, a storm is brewing—only this time it's not because of the looming inciting incident. It's because the protagonist and antagonist are about to collide in such a way that the protagonist

—too "green" and young in the story to stand up to the antagonist—will be thrown off course and make a decision that will cost her dearly.

- Exercise 36. *Using the end of Act One and the midpoint as your tent-pole moments, fill in the gaps to complete the first half of Act Two. Be sure to test all of the scenes you construct.*

For the second half of Act Two, you're going to need to brainstorm three to four key events that push the protagonist down the hill towards the Brick Wall. As always, pay attention to rising conflict. In other words, you want to escalate the opposition—each episode builds on the next and raises the stakes until jeopardy is so high that the protagonist is tempted to abandon the journey and turn back in defeat. Each episode you construct, fueled by the antagonist, causes the MacGuffin to be in jeopardy. But even more than that, these episodes must jeopardize the growth of the protagonist. Throughout the second half of Act Two, you want to push the protagonist to the point that she realizes—or someone else helps her realize—there's nothing to go back to. By the time that moment of self-realization occurs, we as the audience understand completely that everything has changed. There's no turning back. The threshold into Act Three must be crossed, or the story ends. Right here, right now.

- Exercise 37. *Using the midpoint and brick wall as your tent-pole moments, fill in the gap and test your scenes. This segment of your script constitutes the second half of Act Two.*

As soon as the protagonist makes the recommitment to the newly redefined quest, the story will move very quickly. The race is on to the final face-off. From a writing perspective, this translates into the need to be economic with your scenes. You want to pack the biggest punch without getting lost in the mundane. In Act Three, you have nothing to set up. Rather you focus on "paying off" all of the story lines you've been working to set up earlier in your script. Actually, this is a good time to read back through your step outline and identify all of the story elements that beg to be completed. Nothing is more dissatisfying to an audience than an intriguing story line that suddenly disappears.

I prefer, as do most writers, a short and snappy third act. This translates to a maximum of twenty-five to twenty-seven pages (ie., the equivalent of twenty-five to twenty-seven minutes). We're generally looking at ten scenes. Begin with the commitment the protagonist made in order to pull down the brick wall. What plan does that commitment demand? How might it take shape on screen? The antagonist, too, is preparing for the end. Perhaps a shocking reversal is in sight. Whatever the case may be, your protagonist will likely come very close to achieving her goal when she realizes it's a trap—the antagonist has her cornered. She has to summon up everything she has learned over the course of the journey to "dig deep down," as Blake Snyder puts it, and confront the antagonist. (In the case of a romantic comedy, this is the love-interest.)

Continue to keep in mind Hal Ackerman's red-light rule, and look back over the exercises you completed during the first part of this course. It won't take you much effort to isolate the protagonist and guide her from the break into Act Three to the final face-off. When that scene is complete and the stakes of the entire story are finally resolved, all that's left is to drop into the resolution and "fade out." That said, don't drag it out. In crossing over to Act Three, the protagonist made a commitment. Perhaps she had a plan. That plan can be articulated now. And she should make good progress on it until she comes up against a significant push-back from the antagonist. Maybe she realizes it's a trap. Isolated and alone, the protagonist must face off against the antagonist. And, based on the outcome of that face-off, we have the resolution.

◆ Exercise 38. *This is it: The final push. Finish your step outline.*

Congratulations! Not only have you completed your first draft of the step outline, you also possess the necessary skills to troubleshoot and revise it until you're ready to write scenes.

STEP 18. STORYTELLING ETHICS

Tell us a good story and we'll follow you anywhere.

That's why I'd like to hit the pause button today before you jump in to writing your draft. For those of you who aren't yet familiar with it, I'll begin by recapping my 2014 TEDx on story.

Imagine...

It's a beautiful day in Ireland. The waves lap back and forth against the rocks on the shore and the wind tosses the grasses around on the sand dunes. Throughout the bay and around the Giant's Causeway, seals and sea lions drag themselves up on the rocks to sunbathe or frolic in the sea foam. For once, the rain isn't coming down in sheets and you don't have to worry about being swept off your feet into the ocean. (That actually happens in Ireland; no lie.)

Beyond the sand dunes, green fields reflect the sunlight and cows happily swoosh their tails back and forth as they munch on the lush grass. Beyond the field, just on the other side of a wooden fence, there sits a cute yellow bungalow with a bright blue door. Behind that door lives Slattery the Poodle. Ever since he was a wee standard poodle pup, Slattery has had a call to greatness. He has dreamed of one thing and one thing only: to be a farm dog. So, every Sunday morning, he lurks. He stalks that loosely guarded bright blue door. He paces back and forth, waiting for the opportune moment. You see, Slattery knows that, sooner or later, one of the children who live in the house will leave the door ajar, be it ever so slightly. And when they do, he sticks his shiny black nose in the crack and... he's off! One giant ball of black fluff bolts across the backyard. He clears the wooden fence like a jumper pony and, within seconds, reaches the startled cows. In the blink of an eye, he has them running in a perfect stampede circle, as if he has been training for this moment his whole life. What happens next is even more entertaining. Out of the house flies a ball of bright fuchsia. That would be my mother in her very bright pink nightie and Wellington boots. She leaps over the fence even faster than the poodle and darts across the field, arms waving. That image of my childhood is firmly ingrained in my mind. Now, for better or worse, it's ingrained in yours as well. That's because you've just experienced a phenomenon known as *neural coupling*.

We've all been in those boring meetings. You know the ones. The presenter drones on and on in a monotonous voice, flips through PowerPoint slides composed in itty bitty font—where do they get that font?—and slowly but surely, we drift off. That's because the speaker is literally speaking parts of your brain to sleep. You see, when you hear a profusion of facts (or read them or, even, have them projected at you), the information is processed in the language-processing center of your brain. However, when you imagine a giant fluffy black poodle leaping over a fence and running across the field to chase cows, the part of your brain that processes motion fires up. And if I were to tell you that the sea breeze smells of the ocean and I could literally taste the salt on my lips, the parts of your brain that process smell and taste roll up their sleeves and get to work. And so on. You get the picture. Stories, when they're well told, have the power to jump-start our brains.

There's more. Researchers led by Uri Hasson have found there is a negligible difference between the parts of the brain that work when I'm telling the story (reliving the memory, so to speak) and the parts of the brain working when someone watches, hears or reads the story. For all intents and purposes, our brains are mirroring each other—and there's virtually no difference in the way our brains act to process the story whether we're hearing someone else tell it, or are relishing a memory from our own past. What this means is that stories have the power to connect us like nothing else. Great conversations result in a kind of mind-meld. That's one of the reasons why sharing stories brings people together and, as Jerome

Bruner stated in the mid 1980s, why we're twenty-two times more likely to remember a story than facts alone.

The implications for screenwriting and other forms of storytelling are immense. As you craft your scenes, bring in movement, sounds and smells to add dynamism. You'll notice THE TUDORS (2007) often depicts King Henry moving through the set as he engages in important discussions, all the while adding to the esthetics of the scene and engaging our attention. It's also important to think about what you choose to depict on-screen, because we know your readers and viewers will process that information almost exactly as if they were there themselves. I'm not suggesting you not take on difficult stories like SCHINDLER'S LIST (1993). Rather, I'm suggesting that we writers must pay attention to what we choose to leave off-screen and imply. As confirmed by scientific research, the viewer's brain will not process the information to which the viewer is exposed as if it's "just a story." Nor will the story elements to which we've been exposed go away when we turn the television off, or remove a VR headset. Thanks to mirror neurons, the experiences remain firmly engrained in our minds and memories. I believe every content or story creator has a responsibility towards those consuming their art, to think about stewarding that experience, and to pledge, in a sense, to do no harm.

Insanely great stories have the power to bring us together or tear us apart. They transcend geographical and temporal boundaries and oftentimes go so far as to render social classes obsolete. Thus, storytellers have the power to shape the future by rewriting the narrative of our culture, inheriting from the past, and bequeathing renewed traditions to the future. Stories are the great levers of the world—not because they erode our differences, but because they transcend them.

There's more to great storytelling than the power of connection fostered by neural coupling. As researchers led by Paul Zak have shown, there's a close connection between story and the building of empathy. Stories have the power to alter our brain chemistry. When we experience anxiety along with a protagonist, this actually triggers the release of the stress hormone cortisol into our own bloodstream.

We might as well be on screen living the adventure right along with the characters. The key to creating an emotional connection with the character or issue at stake is the release of a second chemical: oxytocin. This is the chemical associated with bonding, caring, and empathy. Zak's research corroborates what expert storytellers from Aristotle, to pioneers in the movie industry, have understood for a long time. To make audiences care about something, you have to adopt a carefully crafted dramatic structure. ("Make me care" is one of Andrew Stanton's key storytelling rules.)

As it turns out, traditional three-act structure, complete with the dramatic character arc, is the key to provoking the release of oxytocin. By following a protagonist who gets called on an adventure, wrestles and struggles to overcome rising conflict, and eventually faces off against the antagonist in the ultimate climax, you've created a basic story structure with a beginning, middle, and end. The protagonist grows and evolves over the course of this testing and experiences the dramatic arc. She isn't in the same place at the end of the story as where we found her at the beginning. Thanks to developments in neuroscience and cognitive psychology research, we're now able to prove scientifically what Aristotle and other great creative minds knew instinctively. Human beings are hardwired for story and we find ourselves thrust into the action through the structure of the three-act narrative. I've outlined for you the process of constructing this type of story in the preceding chapters. I also recommend you check out Lisa Cron's *Wired for Story* to delve deeper into the process of how writers can empower their techniques based on discoveries about how the human brain works.

I believe Zak's research corroborates another powerful key to storytelling that many of us know by instinct. Notice how basic exposition provokes no empathy at all? For example, when we see someone strolling along or even just chatting amiably with a friend—without any kind of struggle to overcome in the scene—we're not confronted with the cues that trigger our brains to react.

Have you ever wondered why the three-act structure is so powerful? I believe it's because the three-act structure, when it is well executed, pits two types of worlds face to face. On one hand, we have the ordinary world, ruled by what we have called the "dominant values." On the other, we have the world as it could be, championed by the "underdog values." In classic hero's quest narratives (such as STAR WARS), we cheer for the protagonist because he represents a world and set of values in which we desperately want to believe. Good triumphs over evil; freedom trumps oppression; hope vanquishes fear. This two-world face-off is true of romantic comedies, adventure stories and all kinds of narratives.

In writing your draft, it's not just about confronting your own desire to create and entertain. As a storyteller, you're also called to communicate to the world something you believe in, something that's worth the audience's time, something that can help us experience some aspect of being human differently—if only ever so slightly. And that brings us to the question of storytelling ethics. There's a reason every story and screenwriting course I've taught to university students or workshop participants includes an adventure into the "great books" tradition, from Plato and Aristotle to Marie de France, Shakespeare and Tolstoy.

Writers and story designers gain an immeasurable richness in their outlook by conversing with other creative minds, whether alive today or living on through the works they created. This process provides insight not only into the craft, but also the recurring questions human beings pose about the world and their existence with remarkable consistency. By reading and steeping ourselves in the storytelling traditions of the past, writers learn to understand their place within history, rather than positioning ourselves (falsely) as pure innovators. For example, medieval authors like Marie de France, Chrétien de Troyes and Dante saw themselves as inheritors of bygone traditions, yet still relevant in their own times. "The ancients wrote obscurely," proclaims Marie de France at the beginning of her *Lais*, "so that we, the moderns, might come along and gloss the letter, thereby revealing the meaning in the text." Twelfth- and thirteenth-century storytellers saw it as their duty to make sense of what they had inherited from the past.

This process of translation and transmission, known to specialists as *translatio*, is not a zero-sum game. The role of the innovator is to bring some added value to the conversation or story. This is how, for example, we got from simple oral traditions about King Arthur and the Knights of the Round Table to a plethora of medieval stories about quests for the Holy Grail and, in turn, the works of such literary giants as Thomas Mallory, Alfred Tennyson and T.H. White. Medieval storytellers took seriously their role as story designers. They inherited blueprints and models from the past, built upon and developed those models, and contributed them to the future. (Back then stories were going through as many redesigns as the iPhone does today.) Given what we've already discussed about neural coupling and brain chemistry, today's story designers have a serious duty to decide what kinds of narratives we turn over to our peers and bequeath to posterity.

When I first read Elie Wiesel's *Night*, I was struck by how it impacted me emotionally. Sometimes I would close the book at night and tears would stream down my face. I felt as if I'd been to the Nazi concentration camps with Wiesel. I was, of course, experiencing first-hand the kind of release of cortisol and oxytocin discussed by Zak. And through neural coupling, I had for all intents and purposes been right there in the death camps. I'd lived alongside the protagonist and experienced his struggles. His memories were imprinted in my brain as strongly as any moments I've lived in "real" life.

There are innumerable stories that need to be passed on…some are more suitable for adults, and others for children, no doubt. I've shared with you some of the more current research on the effects of story so that you can decide what kind of writer and storyteller you will be.

In the *Nicomachean Ethics*, Aristotle advises us to have discussions about what the good entails so that we might better strive for it. I am proposing that we storytellers, too, must care about discussing such boundaries and ask ourselves: "What is the greater good? How does it impact my project? How can I be responsible and ethical in the telling of this story?" As story designers, we can no longer ignore the potential impact of our projects. The greatest thinkers throughout history have contemplated the weight storytellers must carry on their shoulders: With great power comes great responsibility, to borrow one of my favorite lines from SPIDER-MAN.

Plato shared similar concerns in his *Republic* long ago. He went so far as to kick the storytellers out of his ideal city-state, precisely because they had the power to corrupt minds. Check out some of the Nazi propaganda from World War II and I'm willing to bet you will come to some degree of agreement with Plato. However, we often forget that Plato doesn't dismiss the storytellers altogether. After banishing them from the Republic, I would argue he rehabilitates them in his next work, the *Timaeus*. There, Plato's narrator recounts the myth of Atlantis and admonishes us to understand the power of story. The message of the myth is simple: Without stories, we are but children. Stories withstand the tests of time and natural disasters—provided we record them. And when we do, civilizations may rise and fall but the power of story lives on. Plato rehabilitates storytelling in the *Timaeus* because he understands it to be the most powerful vehicle for showcasing ideas in motion. What we believe in theory, we can see played out in story. Story is the canvas against which we test our character, grow, and evolve. Story is the key to cultural memory, and to our future.

Moreover, Plato hints that the truth of a story doesn't always hinge on fact (although there's a place for that, too). Rather, a story can be true because of the truth it points us towards. Thus WALL-E (2008) is true because it tells a story of love and friendship, even though it has no direct corroboration with fact and is set (like the Atlantis myth) in an imaginary world, distant in time from us. Whether the city of Atlantis ever existed or not is beside the point. How many stories have been lost to the mists of time simply because we didn't write them down? Stories, whether recorded in books or on film, are the treasures of experience.

The stories we tell shape the lives we live. They call us to either be part of something greater than ourselves or to sink into the abyss of drudgery. Only you can decide what kind of storyteller you'll become. I hope that, like so many great storytellers before you, you'll choose to be an apprentice to the voices of the past and that, before designing your insanely great tale, you'll pause to ask how humanity stands to be the better for it. Your story will matter, whether that's because it teaches us to look at ourselves differently or it simply invites us to laugh and take ourselves less seriously.

STEP 19. TO DRAFT!

It's time for the vomit draft. Charming.

That's what most writers like to call the first draft, and for good reason. There's no way your first draft will be your last—not if you want to write an insanely great screenplay. The key is to get this first draft out as quickly as possible. You're probably averaging no less than forty, closer to sixty, and no more than seventy scenes in your outline (that would be a lot). At this point, you don't need the scenes you write to be perfect. You just want to get your ideas down on paper. Whether you elect to write one scene a day, ten pages a week, or settle on some other goal, it's time to sit down with your calendar and block out a realistic timeline. Whatever you do, I recommend taking no longer than twelve weeks. Otherwise, you may never get through with the first draft. Deadlines are good. You don't have to write scenes in order, although I prefer to do that. For me, there's something about following the story in the order in which my readers and viewers will encounter it that fuels my creativity. Here's my typical schedule for pushing through the draft:

Day 1: Fade In to page five

Day 2: Finish the setup and complete the Inciting Incident

Days 3-4: Complete Act One

Days 5-6: Push through the first half of Act Two

Days 7-8: Push through the second half of Act Two

Days 9-10: Complete Act Three

Before going any further, you can use the form below to outline your schedule. Then, you can get started on your Day 1 goals!

- Exercise 39. *Fill out your projected writing schedule below.*

  - Day 1
    - Date:

    - Goal:

  - Day 2
    - Date:

    - Goal:

  - Day 3
    - Date:

    - Goal:

  - Day 4
    - Date:

    - Goal:

  - Day 5
    - Date:

Basics of Story Design

- Goal:

- Day 6
  - Date:
  - Goal:

- Day 7
  - Date:
  - Goal:

- Day 8
  - Date:
  - Goal:

- Day 9
  - Date:
  - Goal:

- Day 10
  - Date:
  - Goal:

Adjust your schedule as necessary, but whatever you do, keep pushing forward. If your day job makes it impossible for you to sit down and write so much at one time, commit to writing one scene a day, or pick twelve days that correspond to days off that you can dedicate more fully to your writing. They don't have to be consecutive. Do what works best for you. You can do this—one step at a time, one scene at a time.

STEP 20. THE REWRITE

If you're reading this, you've completed the first draft of your screenplay. Congratulations!

If you haven't, read no further in this chapter until you're done with your draft, and then you can come back to this point. With the first draft behind you, there's major cause to celebrate. This is also where the real work begins. First, I recommend that you take some time off. Go out to the movies, take the dog for a walk or do whatever it is you most enjoy and find relaxing. You've earned it. When you're fully recuperated, step away from your script. I mean it —back off. No submitting to competitions, no contacting agents and for the time being, no sending it out for a reader's opinion. If you're itching to get back to writing, the very best thing you can do right now, especially if you're a first-time screenwriter, is to write another project. That's right: Start the process over again. Go back to the first step and get to work. Brainstorm your new story and characters, go through the exercises and construct your beats and outline. When I started writing movies, a wise mentor told me I'd really hit my stride and have a better idea of what I was doing once I was writing my fifth script. He was right. The thing is, you've learned so much in the past few weeks and you've had the opportunity to test out that learning by writing scenes. Don't worry about the sophistication of your script for now. You need to step away from the project long enough that you can view what you have written objectively through the distant lens of time, with as little emotional attachment as possible. As you progress in your screenplay skills, you'll be able to detach more and more quickly, until you're able to take industry notes and turn around a rewrite in two to four weeks. But for now, it's about doing the invisible work that will help turn you into a great writer. So let's say you design a whole new project and complete the draft. What then? Hopefully a couple of months have passed since you set aside your first project. Perhaps, even, in the process of writing your second script, you've unearthed another story that's begging to be told. If that's the case, go for it. The more time you take away before beginning the first rewrite process, the better. (Of course, you don't want to wait too long, either.)

Here we are, then, ready to think about the rewrite. The first step is to look at your script as objectively as possible. Personally, without looking at my original outline, I like to take the script I created back down to the step outline phase. Chances are it changed quite a bit while I was writing. Then for each scene, I run through a few questions to troubleshoot.

◆ Exercise 40. *Take a close look at the revised step outline.*

> 1. Be sure to include the slug line for each scene and a brief summary of the action. If you like, include a key line of dialogue.
> 2. Identify any story holes. Are there any setups or loose ends that never pay off? Are there any events or actions that take place that haven't been correctly set up? Are any of the major beats missing from your outline? If so, correct the structure immediately.
> 3. Verify that each scene has a setup, event and outcome. How could you heighten the tension for each of these parts of the scene?
> 4. Does the scene stay on spine (i.e., does it contribute to our understanding of the protagonist)? If cutting to the antagonist, a good rule of thumb is not to spend more than three pages away from the protagonist at a time.
> 5. What is the character's desire line going into the scene? What obstacles stand in her way? (Remember that, on

average, we want three obstacles to oppose the character's desire in the course of the scene.)

6. Flag unnecessary backstory and exposition. Brainstorm more effective and interesting ways to introduce the audience to such information if it is indeed necessary. Remember: *Show, don't tell.*

7. What is the central conflict of the scene? If the scene does not contribute to rising conflict, it has no reason for existing. Cut it or find the conflict. Eliminate all coincidences.

You'll notice in the exercise above, I asked you to troubleshoot for story holes and coincidences. It's very common in writing a first draft that a writer might begin a story line and not carry it through to completion. At other times, perhaps something is allowed to happen without any apparent set up. Everything must have a reason. In GLADIATOR, for example, we believe Commodus is capable of fighting Maximus in the arena because we have seen that he is an expert swordsman—near the beginning we see the young Commodus training out in the snow as Maximus walks through the camp. In troubleshooting for the rewrite, it's very important to make sure that every major development is set up at least once (and twice is even better).

Keeping that in mind, I find it useful to construct a character arc for each of the main characters. I do this by pulling out the scenes that contribute to their development and creating a little summary of their evolution through the movie. If at any time the character evolves without having to struggle their way out of a sticky situation —for example they simply wake up and have changed their mind about an important issue—I've identified a moment of *jumping conflict* that must be remedied. I can flag those kinds of problems and get back to brainstorming how to fix them. Ideally, each step my character takes forward must be hard earned. The character makes choices and takes chances without any guarantee as to outcome.

- Exercise 41. *Draft the character arc for each of your main characters.*

Do this for at least the protagonist, supporting character and antagonist. Identify any potential moments of jumping conflict. Brainstorm ways in which you can make their growth more believable or more interesting.

- Exercise 42. *Looking more closely at the protagonist now, verify the strength of your forty-minute and sixty-minute character points. (If you don't remember the purpose of these beats, go back to Step 7.) Brainstorm ways to make these transitions in the character arc even better. As always: Show, don't tell.*

I also like to revisit the relationship between the protagonist and antagonist. I find it helpful to place them in proximity two times prior to the final face-off in Act Three. This doesn't mean they have to come face-to-face, although oftentimes they will. Perhaps, instead, the protagonist sees the antagonist from afar, as Luke Skywalker sees Darth Vader before he strikes down his old mentor. Whether or not the story allows for the protagonist and antagonist to actually meet prior to the climax in Act Three, the protagonist and audience must feel the antagonist's presence in order to set up the ultimate encounter.

- Exercise 43. *Identify two encounters or almost-encounters in Acts One and Two that help set up the tension and dynamic between the protagonist and antagonist. (Obviously, if you're writing a romantic comedy, these characters will spend a lot of time together.) Brainstorm ways in which you can make it even more difficult for the protagonist to defeat the antagonist. How does the antagonist box in the protagonist through difficult situations from which the protagonist must fight her way out?*

Finally, a few words about dialogue (a topic to which we will return in more detail in a later volume). For now, focus on economizing dialogue. Cut down adjectives and adverbs. If you listen to yourself speak, you'll realize that we don't use these additional "describing words" as much as you might first imagine. If you find your writing is heavy on adverbs, pick a better verb. If it's heavy on adjectives, pick a better noun—trim, trim and when you've trimmed, trim some more. You'll also want to play around with ways in which to make the true meaning slide into *subtext*. That's just a fancy way of saying the character means something other than what he or she says. For example, let's say a father and son have just reconciled. Perhaps they don't like to talk about their feelings. The sooner this whole affair can be water under the bridge, the better. In an effort to show his love for his son, rather than speak his emotions out loud, the father has bought a pair of tickets for them to watch his son's favorite baseball team.

>
> DAD
> We don't have all day. Unless, of course, you want to miss the first pitch.
>
> SON
> I love you too, dad.

The son reads between the lines. By taking him to the game, his father is expressing his love. So, without further ado, he calls him out: "I love you too, dad."

We have another example of this economy of dialogue (ad-libbed on set by Harrison Ford) in the epic climax of STAR WARS V: THE EMPIRE STRIKES BACK. As he's led to the freezing chamber, Leia calls out to Han: "I love you." He replies: "I know." Although urban legend has it that Harrison Ford had to fight Lucas to keep this line in the script, I much prefer it to the alternative—"I love you, too." The "I know" communicates a depth of feelings between Han and Leia. He doesn't need her to voice her emotions to him because he has seen it all along. And it gives the audience an even more dramatic payoff when he finally voices his love for her in STAR WARS VI: RETURN OF THE JEDI (1983).

Another nifty trick to good dialogue is allowing the thrust and parry to turn on key phrases. Say we have a character named Martin, who is really frustrated with his fiancée, Sheila. They have just recently moved in together. Meanwhile, Sheila has been spending all her time decorating for their first holiday as a couple—and spending a great deal of Martin's hard-earned cash. To her, the carefully selected tree skirt is an expression of love. To him, it's a nightmare devised to ruin his bachelor pad. Sheila can sense something's wrong and keeps nagging him. Meanwhile Martin is on the verge of losing his mind.

> SHEILA
> Maybe I should have put the tree over in that corner. We could move it in the morning.
> MARTIN
> Enough of the Tree. Look at this place. It's like the North Pole in here. I can't do this.
> SHEILA
> What's that supposed to mean. Where are you—
> MARTIN
> Don't wait up.

When Sheila mentions moving the "tree," Martin loses it. He picks up the word and turns it back against her, adding a ubiquitous "I can't do this anymore." Sheila responds at first by assuming he means Christmas and the decorations. She attempts to win him over by reminding Martin it's the "most wonderful time of the year." Suddenly, it hits her—"what does that mean?" Note how we don't have to indicate that Martin grabs his jacket or gets off the couch. The actor can tell this from the fact that Sheila asks Martin where he's going. Instead of answering her question, he tells her not to wait up. Clearly, their relationship is on the rocks. It's unclear what's going to happen. Once again, economy of dialogue allows us to create powerful and meaningful subtext. My friend Linda Seger's *Writing Subtext: What Lies Beneath* can be a useful resource for flexing this writing muscle.

Basics of Story Design

- Exercise 44. *Pick one scene you deem particularly good. Now rewrite it, paying special attention to economy of dialogue. As you execute your rewrite, be sure to repeat this process for each scene.*

By working beneath the surface to eliminate story holes and strengthen character growth, you'll be sure to make the most out of your second draft. Then and only then, you might consider submitting your screenplay to a professional reader for feedback or to a competition.

- Exercise 45. *I'm going to recommend one final checklist to make sure your scenes have the elements they need in order to function or "turn." Run this series of diagnostic tests anytime you're seeking to make a scene better. As you execute your rewrite, be sure to repeat this process for each scene.*

   1. What is the setup?
   2. What is the desire line of the character driving the scene?
   3. What are three main obstacles that enter into conflict with that desire line in the scene?
   4. What is the main event of the scene?
   5. How does your character respond?
   6. How do others characters respond, and how does the tension continue to rise?
   7. What is the outcome of the scene? (This is the perfect opportunity to drop a memorable line of dialogue.)

Remember, your invisible work will pay off. Success never happens overnight. It's the result of hard work, sustained over time. And whatever you do, keep on writing!

APPENDIX: DOCUMENTARY FILM

What about other kinds of stories... do the same principles apply?

You bet they do. That's the great aspect of story design. Now that you understand the building blocks at play in some of the greatest stories ever written, you can think about how to apply these techniques, or tools, to other forms of storytelling. This is possible because those of us who study the underlying principles of great screenwriting or storytelling aren't inventing it from scratch. Rather, we're noting recurring principles in the great stories we consume. Once we spot those trends and characteristics, it's possible to think about how to replicate them and ensure the key ingredients of success get included in our own tales.

The first person to note these kinds of trends and write about them was Aristotle, who outlined the basic principles of dramatic narrative, as he saw them, in his *Poetics*. For Aristotle, plot and character are the two most significant elements of great storytelling. Special effects come in last. That's not because they're not enjoyable, it's because the effects will never compensate adequately for a lack of story. You can blow things up all day long—if the plot (and character) development elements required to solicit the emotions of the reader or audience aren't present, you're fighting a losing battle. Take STAR WARS IV: A NEW HOPE, or WONDER WOMAN, for example. The special effects are amazing, but they don't supplant or attempt to replace very real stakes and jeopardy. The dramatic premise, the fight between good and evil is real and palpable, and it plays out through the characters and their own internal struggles on an entirely human scale.

I'd argue that story design principles can serve you equally well in the creation of short films, short stories, novels, and even story-driven commercials, but those are discussions for another day. In this appendix, by popular demand, I'll briefly overview how to apply them to the crafting of an insanely great documentary film.

In recent years, the world of documentary filmmaking has exploded. Rapidly evolving advances in technology have broken down barriers to entry and made it more possible than ever to tell important stories to massive audiences. That said, as you now know, not all stories are created equal.

A video of my neighbor's cat might elicit the pleasure of thousands of Facebook viewers for a few days, but much more focused groundwork and preparation needs to be done in order to craft a meaningful documentary film that connects with audiences on an emotional level, and incites viewers to action.

Of course, impact has many faces. Some films spark community conversations. Others scale dialogue to national, and even global, spheres of influence. For example, THE INVISIBLE WAR (2012) introduced twenty pieces of new legislation to address the U.S. Military sexual assault epidemic. A SMALL ACT (2010) inspired donations of over $2 million to high school education programs in Kenya. AMERICAN PROMISE (2013) has already been used by 15,000 educators through the Teaching Tolerance curriculum, and CRIME AFTER CRIME (2011) raised over $160,000 for domestic violence prevention organizations across the United States. Other notable films like AN INCONVENIENT TRUTH (2006) initiated ongoing, global conversations about climate change.

Making audiences care—and not simply exposing them to foreign worlds and realities—has been in the DNA of documentary filmmaking for a very long time. The early filmmakers of the twentieth century quickly moved beyond creating anthropological records of foreign cultures and events and sought to influence and shape culture. They were, to all intents and purposes, some of the earliest social entrepreneurs, who understood the power of the media and storytelling to effect change. I believe that is, to a great extent, what it means to be a socially conscious artist. We push ourselves daily to shed new light on the world in which we live, and go so far as to expose problems or inspire others, by sharing experiences of great joy. We tell stories with the primary goal of making others care... and in the best case scenario, we aspire to bring about actual, real-life change. By planning intentional, researched, scalable impact campaigns around a documentary film, twenty-first century storytellers are harnessing new and exciting developments in technology—from digital film to virtual reality experiences—as well as advances in storytelling research, in order to reach broader audiences and effect change.

How do documentarians connect with viewers and make audiences care? At the end of the day, as Andrew Stanton reminds us, that's the end-all-be-all of every story. Maya Angelou has her own way of putting it: "People won't remember what you said, they'll remember how you made them feel." In my own work, I've never approached documentary storytelling from the position that it's about communicating facts. Rather, like most documentarians today, I want to make audiences care about the issues at stake and, even better, take action of some kind (and preferably curate that action or empower it through the impact campaign surrounding the film).

We've already noted Jerome Bruner's point that we remember stories twenty-two times more than facts. We've also discussed how certain aspects of stories and the ways in which we tell them release chemicals into our brains and actually change the chemical balance of our bodies. Oxytocin and cortisol trigger attachment, stress and (together) emotional investment and vulnerability. Dopamine, released when we encounter new information or see something from a fresh perspective, acts like a save button in our brains. There you have it: the OCD of insanely great storytelling. (You'll find links to both my 2014 and 2015 TEDx talks on these subjects, "Hardwired for Story" and "Write and Wrong," at basicsofstorydesign.com.)

We even know that three-act structure is the most effective way to gain the investment of a viewer and trigger these kinds of reactions. As I made the transition into the world of documentary filmmaking, I wanted to think about how three-act structure could be reimagined and adapted to the needs of the documentary and impact world. In other words, what does it look like for a documentary film to have an effective beginning, middle and end? How might documentary filmmakers adapt the techniques proven effective in narrative feature film writing in order to sustain the interest and engagement of audiences? (And, ultimately, make the message "stick" so well that it carries beyond the theatre and into measurable action and impact?)

The key is to pose the question, who do we want to go through the greatest character arc as they watch the documentary film? What is the actual effect we're hoping to achieve? For me, the answer is simple. Whether there's a protagonist in the film itself or not (due to a more issues-based approach—although I prefer the former), the unity and integrity of the documentary film experience aims to provoke a character arc in each member of the audience. Ultimately, I want an audience member to enter the theatre or sit down in front of their television with the sum of knowledge and perceptions they have about the world, and I want the film to invite that person on a journey in which they become an active participant, and shift their perspective so that they are ready to take action when the film ends. It's that simple. **In a great documentary film, the audience experiences the highs and lows of the story design process because the audience member is the protagonist.** At least, that's how I like to think about it.

With all of that in mind, here's my story design process adapted to mapping out a documentary film. It's helpful to think about these issues prior to filming, but the primary intent here is for you to be empowered to assemble the edit so as to achieve a strong character arc with a solid beginning, middle and end. I've used these techniques to counsel and consult with numerous documentary teams, as well as polish up the films I've written and produced, and I think you'll find useful ways to build on their foundation and make them your own.

- **Point of Attack.** This is the beginning of your movie. Like the writer of a feature film, you'll want to try a few options in order to pick a scene that best introduces the premise and themes of the project. Remember to showcase the values at stake in the story world. You're setting up the world as it currently exists, and in which your issue mandates a shift (e.g., our world is one in which the trafficking of human beings represents one of the most dynamic, growing economies, and this should not be the case—everyone deserves to be free). The goal here is to provide an opportunity for your audience to identify with the underdog values of the documentary world, even if they don't know how to get involved to make a change. (Your impact campaign will provide next-step actions.)

o When writing a great documentary film, setting up a clear A vs. B values system is key, just like in a great feature film. Too many documentarians fall prey to "more is more" and end up with A vs. B, and C vs. D, but also E vs. F. Instead of multiple sets of (unrelated) conflicting values, think in terms of **nesting values**. The *internal, external,* and *philosophical* (and perhaps even *theological*) stakes serve as different manifestations and articulations of a single, greater truth. For example, the *internal stakes* shows how the truth plays out in the inner journey of a key character. Then, the *external stakes* reveal how that inner journey is in conflict with the dominant values of the realm or society in which the story plays out. The *philosophical stakes* remind us of what is at stake in the world and society at large—our world as viewers—if the dominant values win out. And for me, the *theological stakes* express what happens on the scale of humankind (not just society). Your various stakes will ideally nest just as Luke's internal journey (will he become a Jedi or not?), the external stakes (will the rebellion defeat the empire?), the philosophical stakes (will freedom win out over tyranny?), and the theological stakes (will good triumph over evil?) come together to form a single, comprehensive strand in STAR WARS.

- **The World as We Know It, or the Ordinary World.** It's time to build a **sequence** (series of scenes) to introduce the audience to the issue. Remember: *Show, don't tell.* In the world of documentary film, actions and interactions are still more powerful than background and exposition. Don't get lost in the facts. Introduce your audience to the issue through the lives of the characters featured in your documentary. Pay special attention to the dominant values of the documentary world. Give the audience time to get to know the characters and featured experts who'll guide us along the journey. Can't escape from the world of talking heads? Of course you can. Consider the possibilities that animation might introduce into your project. Get creative. It's all about finding an effective way to engage the viewer.

- As part of the **ordinary world**, you'll want to signal that **a storm is brewing**. Things may appear to be continuing on as usual, but you want to create the impression that something is about to happen. Things can't continue as they are. You're setting up the opportunity for an event to take place that invites the protagonist—in this case your audience—into a new journey. In some cases, you're getting ready to open up the new promise of possibility: a possibility for change. Or, if you're deep diving into a challenging issue that's much worse in reality than the audience imagines, you're about to take them down the rabbit hole into the harsh day-to-day realities to which they've managed to remain oblivious and from which they've been sheltered... until now. We want the audience to get the sense that there's something not quite right about the world being presented to us, and we're ready to expose it.

- **Inciting Incident, or Catalyst.** Remember, we're just lighting the fuse here. The stick of dynamite doesn't explode quite yet. This is the moment everything changes, even if the audience is unaware of how crucial the information is. This is the first invitation to go on the journey down the rabbit hole. Introduce a critical, and unexpected, aspect of your story.

- **Dilemma.** Now we're going to up the ante. The stick of dynamite explodes. Here, I want the audience to mentally wrestle with the decision to call into question their assumptions and go on the journey. Position a story element or research to cause the audience to jump off the ledge. How can this be? This shouldn't be possible in the real world. And yet, how can we possibly make a difference? We get the sense that if we continue on with the film, we'll be presented with answers to some of our questions. By this point, the audience *wants* to follow the director down the rabbit hole but is perhaps a little tentative simply because the topic might seem overwhelming.

- **The audience commits to crossing the threshold.** They might not fully understand what they're getting themselves into yet, but you want audience members to be willing participants in the journey. By the time we reach the threshold and the break into Act Two, the audience should have the sense that their perception of the world at the beginning of the film was limited. They want, and need, to learn more. This will ensure that they not only continue watching the film, they'll be emotionally invested in the outcome. You've opened the possibility for more facts and details in the second act, because your audience crosses the threshold seeking answers. We're ready to take the leap.

[End of Act One]

- **Adventure Sequence.** We've dived down the rabbit hole and now we're confronted with the realities of the extraordinary world. This is a space that's quite different from our day-to-day experience. We're discovering new territories and feel a sense of progression and measurable success in confronting the bleak realities of the issue. As in a major feature narrative, it's also a good time to introduce your supporting character or storyline. I find it useful to structure the first half of Act Two with a series of three or four mini-goals to help me get from the threshold crossing all the way to the midpoint. Create topical, nested subdivisions for the first half of Act Two. This is your chance to show the audience just how different reality is compared to the assumptions they had entering the documentary in Act One.

- **Character Moment #1 (around 40%).** This is a great time to solidify the audience's growth by introducing them to an aspect of the story (or statistic) they might not have been willing to consider or hear during Act One. You've earned their good will. Push them further out of the comfort zone. This is a good time to remember that your primary protagonist, for our purposes here, is the audience. We want the audience to go through the character arc. If you also have a secondary protagonist, to help them identify, within the film, this is the moment for their first character moment too.

- **Midpoint. The tide turns**. The midpoint of a great documentary makes utterly clear what's at stake. Here, the audience feels that the underdog values (for which they've been rooting) are under attack. From this point forward, we're overwhelmed with the sense of an uphill battle. It's not going to be as easy as we thought to defeat the dominant, cultural values. In fact, this marks the point when we begin to question whether it will be possible at all.

Basics of Story Design

- **All Downhill: Attack of the Dominant Values.** Everything goes from bad to worse. The second half of Act Two presents a series of ever-increasing setbacks. Not only are we facing an uphill battle, it seems unlikely the underdog values can win. This incites a feeling of outrage in the audience. How can we have allowed things to get so bad? Why can't we change the outcome? What will it take to stand up to the bad guys? Once again, I like to split the second half of Act Two into three to four mini-goals or sequences.

- **Character Moment #2 (around 65%).** This is your opportunity to push the audience even further along. Present them with a fact or experience that they wouldn't have been able to imagine at the beginning of the journey. However, they're willing to confront it now, given everything they've seen this far—even if it makes them feel uncomfortable. They should feel a pit in their stomach by this point of the story—a promise of the brick wall to come. Once again, mirror this experience of the character moment if you have a protagonist figure inside the documentary story, with whom the audience is predisposed to identify and empathize.

- **The Brick Wall.** As in a feature film, the brick wall affords the audience the opportunity to take in the overwhelming horror of the dominant values. For a moment, we feel that fighting back is utterly useless. There's no point. But it's time to allow the film, and the characters in it, to serve as a great supporting character to the audience. Create the equivalent of a pep talk by demonstrating just enough of a glimmer of hope that they're willing to get in the fight and push back. The characters in the film are willing to go where we might fail to go, because they recognize what's a stake and know it's the only way forward. The brick wall in a documentary is perhaps the most critical moment when it comes to inviting your audience to take a stand and commit to not only considering your solution, but joining you in the impact campaign. The Brick Wall marks the end of Act Two and serves as the break into Act Three.

[End of Act 2]

- **The Final Face-Off.** This is your opportunity to envision solutions, even if they seem far-off at the current time. Provide the audience with a glimmer of hope. Present them an image of what the world could be. Show them that victory is possible, even if it hasn't been achieved yet. This is your chance to issue an invitation for viewers to take up and continue the fight into the real world, when the movie ends. In a great impact documentary film, the final face-off typically occurs off-screen. It is achieved by the viewers, together, when they embrace the pathway laid out in the impact campaign. Act Three of the film must make the audience feel that change is not only desirable, it's achievable —even in the face of great adversity. It's why they sign up to be part of the solution.

- **Resolution.** Provide the audience with a sense of how different the world might be, if we all chose to make a difference. This is the vision that will guide the impact campaign. It's never too early to start planning how you want to package the film for the audience. Think of your film as a product, and you'll recognize in my advice the general principles of product design, as described, for example, in Jonah Berger's book, *Contagious: Why Things Catch On*. Jonah wants to know what makes things popular, why people talk about certain products and ideas more than others, and why some stories "go viral" (whereas others do not). It might be tempting to respond that the key lies in advertising—but that's not true. If you're interested in building "viral" content

Basics of Story Design

that others will talk about, endorse, and pass on, it has much more to do with questions asked and choices made at the stage of product development. I'm a fan of applying this approach to documentary films, as they can help guide us towards storytelling decisions that not only make sense for the story, but also for the marketability and share-ability of your film. In other words, don't wait until you've shot your film to figure out what you want to do with it. We'll return to these principles in more detail in a book on documentary filmmaking.

[End of Act 3]

WORKS CITED

About Time (2013). Dir. Richard Curtis. Perfs. Domhnall Gleeson, Rachel McAdams, Bill Nighy. Universal Pictures.

Ackerman, Hal (2003). *Write Screenplays that Sell*. Los Angeles, CA: Tallfellow Press.

Amadeus (1984). Dir. Milos Forman. Perfs. F. Murray Abraham, Tom Hulce, Elizabeth Berridge. Orion Pictures.

American Promise (2013). Dir. Joe Brewster and Michele Stephenson. POV/ PBS.

Aristotle (335 BC). *Poetics*.

Aristotle (384-322 BC). *Metaphysics*.

Aristotle (350 BC). *Nicomachean Ethics*.

As Good As It Gets (1997). Dir. James L. Brooks. Perfs. Jack Nicholson, Helen Hunt, Greg Kinnear. TriStar Pictures.

Berger, Jonah. *Contagious: Why Things Catch On*. New York: Simon & Schuster, 2013.

Braveheart (1995). Dir. Mel Gibson. Perfs. Mel Gibson, Sophie

Marceau, Patrick McGoohan. Icon Entertainment International.

Casablanca (1942). Dir. Michael Cortiz. Perfs. Humphrey Bogart, Ingrid Bergman, Paul Henreid. Warner Brothers Pictures.

Chronicles of Narnia: The Lion, the Witch and the Wardrobe (2005). Dir. Andrew Adamson. Perf. Tilda Swinton, Georgie Henley, William Moseley. Walt Disney Pictures.

Crime after Crime (2011). Dir. Yoav Potasch. Oprah Winfrey Network.

Cron, Lisa (2012). *Wired for Story: The Writer's Guide to Using Brain Science to Hook Readers from the Very First Sentence*. Berkeley, CA: Ten Speed Press.

Dark Knight Rises, The (2012). Dir. Christopher Nolan. Perfs. Christian Bale, Tom Hardy, Anne Hathaway. Warner Brothers Pictures.

Egri, Lajos (1946). *The Art of Dramatic Writing: Its Basis in the Creative Interpretation of Human Motives*. New York, NY: Simon and Schuster.

Finding Nemo (2003). Dir. Andrew Stanton, Lee Unkrich. Perfs. Albert Brooks, Ellen DeGeneres, Alexander Gould. Disney Pixar.

Frozen (2013). Dir. Chris Buck, Jennifer Lee. Perfs. Kristen Bell, Idina Menzel, Jonathan Groff. Walt Disney Pictures.

Gladiator (2000). Dir. Ridley Scott. Perfs. Russell Crowe, Joaquin Phoenix, Connie Nielsen. DreamWorks SKG, Universal Pictures.

Godin, Seth (2007). *The Dip: A Little Book that Teaches You When to Quit (and When to Stick)*. New York: Penguin.

Gravity (2013). Dir. Alfonso Cuarón. Perfs. Sandra Bullock, George Clooney, Ed Harris. Warner Brothers Pictures.

Hauge, Michael (1991). *Writing Screenplays that Sell.* New York, NY: Collins.

How to Train Your Dragon 2 (2014). Dir. Dean DuBlois. Perfs. Jay Baruchel, Cate Blanchett, Gerard Butler. DreamWorks Animation.

An Inconvenient Truth (2006). Dir. Davis Guggenheim. Participant Media.

The Invisible War (2012). Dir. Kirby Dick and Prod. Amy Ziering and Tanner King. Cinedigm Docudrama Films.

Jerry Maguire (1996). Dir. Cameron Crowe. Perfs. Tom Cruise, Cuba Gooding, Jr., Renée Zellweger. TriStar Pictures.

King's Speech, The (2010). Dir. Tom Hooper. Perfs. Colin Firth, Geoffrey Rush, Helena Bonham Carter. Weinstein Company.

Kramer vs. Kramer (1979). Dir. Robert Benton. Perfs. Dustin Hoffman, Meryl Streep, Jane Alexander. Columbia Pictures.

Matrix, The (1999). Dir. Andy Wachowski, Lana Wachowski. Perfs. Keanu Reeves, Laurence Fishburne, Carrie-Anne Moss. Warner Brothers.

Marie de France (fl. 1165). *Lais.*

McKee, Robert (1997). *Story: Substance, Structure, Style and the Principles of Screenwriting.* New York, NY: Regan Books.

Mission Impossible: Ghost Protocol (2011). Dir. Brad Bird. Perfs. Tom

Cruise, Jeremy Renner, Simon Pegg. Paramount Pictures.

Notting Hill (1999). Dir. Roger Michell. Perfs. Hugh Grant, Julia Roberts, Richard McCabe. Polygram Filmed Entertainment.

Patriot, The (2000). Dir. Roland Emmerich. Perfs. Mel Gibson, Heath Ledger, Joely Richardson. Columbia Pictures.

Pirates of the Caribbean: The Curse of the Black Pearl (2003). Dir. Gore Verbinski. Perfs. Johnny Depp, Geoffrey Rush, Orlando Bloom. Walt Disney Pictures.

Plato (360 BC). *The Republic*.

Plato (360 BC). *Timaeus*.

Proposal, The (2009). Dir. Anne Fletcher. Perfs. Sandra Bullock, Ryan Reynolds, Mary Steenburgen. Touchstone Pictures.

Pulp Fiction (1994). Dir. Quentin Tarantino. Perfs. John Travolta, Uma Thurman, Samuel L. Jackson. Miramax.

Raiders of the Lost Ark (1981). Dir. Steven Spielberg. Perfs. Harrison Ford, Karen Allen, Paul Freeman. Paramount Pictures, Lucasfilms.

Rogue One: A Star Wars Story (2016). Dir. Gareth Edwards. Perfs. Felicity Jones, Diego Luna, Donnie Yen, Mads Mikkelsen, Riz Ahmed, Forest Whitaker, James Earl Jones.

Schindler's List (1993). Dir. Steven Spielberg. Perfs. Liam Neeson, Ralph Fiennes, Ben Kingsley. Universal Pictures.

Seger, Linda (2011). *Writing Subtext: What Lies Beneath*. Los Angeles, CA: Michael Wiese Productions.

Shawshank Redemption, The (1994). Dir. Frank Darabont. Perfs. Tim Robbins, Morgan Freeman, Bob Gunton. Castle Rock Entertainment.

Sherlock (2010). Dir. Mark Gatiss, Steven Moffat. Perfs. Benedict Cumberbatch, Martin Freeman, Rupert Graves. Hartswood Films, BBC.

Shakespeare, William (1603). *Macbeth*.

Shrek (2001). Dir. Andrew Adamson, Vicky Jenson. Perfs. Mike Myers, Eddie Murphy, Cameron Diaz. DreamWorks.

Silence of the Lambs, The (1991). Dir. Jonathan Demme. Perfs. Jodie Foster, Anthony Hopkins, Lawrence A. Bonney. Orion Pictures.

Silver Linings Playbook (2012). Dir. David O. Russell. Perfs. Bradley Cooper, Jennifer Lawrence, Robert De Niro. Weinstein Company.

A Small Act (2010). Dir. Jennifer Arnold. HBO Documentary Films.

Snow White and the Huntsman (2012). Dir. Rupert Sanders. Perfs. Kristen Stewart, Chris Hemsworth, Charlize Theron. Universal Pictures.

Snyder, Blake (2005). *Save the Cat: The Last Book on Screenwriting You'll Ever Need*. Los Angeles, CA: Michael Wiese Productions.

Spider-Man (2002). Dir. Sam Raimi. Perfs. Tobey Maguire, Kirsten Dunst, Willem Defoe. Columbia Pictures.

Star Wars Episode IV: A New Hope (1977). Dir. George Lucas. Perfs. Mark Hamill, Harrison Ford, Carrie Fisher. Lucasfilms.

Star Wars Episode V: The Empire Strikes Back (1980). Dir. Irvin Kershner. Perfs. Mark Hamill, Harrison Ford, Carrie Fisher. Lucasfilms.

Star Wars Episode VI: Return of the Jedi (1983). Dir. Richard Marquand. Perfs. Mark Hamill, Harrison Ford, Carrie Fisher. Lucasfilms.

Star Wars Episode VII: The Force Awakens (2015). Dir. J.J. Abrams. Perfs. Mark Hamill, Harrison Ford, Carrie Fisher, Adam Driver, John Boyega, Daisy Ridley. Walt Disney Pictures.

Tangled (2010). Dir. Nathan Greno, Byron Howard. Perfs. Mandy Moore, Zachary Levi, Donna Murphy. Walt Disney Pictures.

Toy Story 3 (2010). Dir. Lee Unkrich. Perfs. Tom Hanks, Tim Allen, Joan Cusack. Walt Disney Pictures/Pixar Animation Studios.

Tudors, The (2007). Dir. Michael Hirst. Perfs. Jonathan Rhys Meyers, Henry Cavill, Anthony Brophy. Peace Arch Entertainment, Showtime Studios.

Up (2009). Dir. Pete Docter, Bob Peterson. Perfs. Edward Asner, Jordan Nagai, John Ratzenberger. Walt Disney Pictures/Pixar Animation Studios.

Vogler, Christopher (1992). *The Writer's Journey: Mythic Structure for Writers*. Los Angeles, CA: Michael Wiese Productions.

WALL-E (2008). Dir. Andrew Stanton. Perfs. Ben Burtt, Elissa Knight, Jeff Garlin. Walt Disney Pictures/Pixar Animation Studios.

Walter, Richard (2010). *Essentials of Screenwriting: The Art, Craft and*

Business of Film and Television Writing. New York, NY: Plume.

West Side Story (1961). Dir. Jerome Robbins, Robert Wise. Perfs. Natalie Wood, George Chakiris, Richard Beymer. Mirisch Corporation, Seven Arts Productions.

Wiesel, Elie (1960). *Night*. First English Edition. New York, NY: Hill & Wang.

Wizard of Oz, The (1939). Dir. Victor Fleming, George Cukor. Perfs. Judy Garland, Frank Morgan, Ray Bolger. Metro-Goldwyn-Mayer.

Wonder Woman (2017). Dir. Patty Jenkins. Perfs. Gal Gadot, Chris Pine, Robin Wright, David Thewlis, Elena Anaya, Connie Nielsen, Danny Huston.